MANHATTAN GMAT

Algebra

GMAT Strategy Guide

This essential guide covers algebra in all its various forms (and disguises) on the GMAT. Master fundamental techniques and nuanced strategies to help you solve for unknown variables of every type.

guide 2

MIX
Paper from
responsible sources
FSC® C014174

Algebra GMAT Strategy Guide, Fifth Edition

10-digit International Standard Book Number: 1-935707-62-0
13-digit International Standard Book Number: 978-1-935707-62-2
eISBN: 978-1-937707-03-3

Note: *GMAT, Graduate Management Admission Test, Graduate Management Admission
Council,* and *GMAC* are all registered trademarks of the Graduate Management Admission
Council, which neither sponsors nor is affiliated in any way with this product.

Layout Design: Dan McNaney and Cathy Huang
Cover Design: Evyn Williams and Dan McNaney
Cover Photography: Alli Ugosoli

INSTRUCTIONAL GUIDE SERIES

SUPPLEMENTAL GUIDE SERIES

MANHATTAN
GMAT

April 24th, 2012

Dear Student,

Thank you for picking up a copy of *Algebra*. I hope this book provides just the guidance you need to get the most out of your GMAT studies.

As with most accomplishments, there were many people involved in the creation of the book you are holding. First and foremost is Zeke Vanderhoek, the founder of Manhattan GMAT. Zeke was a lone tutor in New York when he started the company in 2000. Now, 12 years later, the company has instructors and offices nationwide and contributes to the studies and successes of thousands of students each year.

Our Manhattan GMAT Strategy Guides are based on the continuing experiences of our instructors and students. For this volume, we are particularly indebted to Dave Mahler and Stacey Koprince. Dave deserves special recognition for his contributions over the past number of years. Dan McNaney and Cathy Huang provided their design expertise to make the books as user-friendly as possible, and Noah Teitelbaum and Liz Krisher made sure all the moving pieces came together at just the right time. And there's Chris Ryan. Beyond providing additions and edits for this book, Chris continues to be the driving force behind all of our curriculum efforts. His leadership is invaluable. Finally, thank you to all of the Manhattan GMAT students who have provided input and feedback over the years. This book wouldn't be half of what it is without your voice.

At Manhattan GMAT, we continually aspire to provide the best instructors and resources possible. We hope that you will find our commitment manifest in this book. If you have any questions or comments, please email me at dgonzalez@manhattanprep.com. I'll look forward to reading your comments, and I'll be sure to pass them along to our curriculum team.

Thanks again, and best of luck preparing for the GMAT!

Sincerely,

Dan

Dan Gonzalez
President
Manhattan GMAT

HOW TO ACCESS YOUR ONLINE RESOURCES

If you...

⊙ **are a registered Manhattan GMAT student**

and have received this book as part of your course materials, you have AUTOMATIC access to ALL of our online resources. This includes all practice exams, question banks, and online updates to this book. To access these resources, follow the instructions in the Welcome Guide provided to you at the start of your program. Do NOT follow the instructions below.

⊙ **purchased this book from the Manhattan GMAT online store or at one of our centers**

1. Go to: www.manhattanprep.com/gmat/studentcenter.

2. Log in using the username and password used when your account was set up.

⊙ **purchased this book at a retail location**

1. Create an account with Manhattan GMAT at the website: www.manhattanprep.com/gmat/register.

2. Go to: www.manhattanprep.com/gmat/access.

3. Follow the instructions on the screen.

Your one year of online access begins on the day that you register your book at the above URL.

You only need to register your product ONCE at the above URL. To use your online resources any time AFTER you have completed the registration process, log in to the following URL: www.manhattanprep.com/gmat/studentcenter.

Please note that online access is nontransferable. This means that only NEW and UNREGISTERED copies of the book will grant you online access. Previously used books will NOT provide any online resources.

⊙ **purchased an eBook version of this book**

1. Create an account with Manhattan GMAT at the website: www.manhattanprep.com/gmat/register.

2. Email a copy of your purchase receipt to gmat@manhattanprep.com to activate your resources. Please be sure to use the same email address to create an account that you used to purchase the eBook.

For any technical issues, email techsupport@manhattanprep.com or call 800-576-4628.

Please refer to the following page for a description of the online resources that come with this book.

YOUR ONLINE RESOURCES

Your purchase includes ONLINE ACCESS to the following:

⊙ 6 Computer-Adaptive Online Practice Exams

The 6 full-length computer-adaptive practice exams included with the purchase of this book are delivered online using Manhattan GMAT's proprietary computer-adaptive test engine. The exams adapt to your ability level by drawing from a bank of more than 1,200 unique questions of varying difficulty levels written by Manhattan GMAT's expert instructors, all of whom have scored in the 99th percentile on the Official GMAT. At the end of each exam you will receive a score, an analysis of your results, and the opportunity to review detailed explanations for each question. You may choose to take the exams timed or untimed.

The content presented in this book is updated periodically to ensure that it reflects the GMAT's most current trends and is as accurate as possible. You may view any known errors or minor changes upon registering for online access.

Important Note: The 6 computer adaptive online exams included with the purchase of this book are the SAME exams that you receive upon purchasing ANY book in the Manhattan GMAT Complete Strategy Guide Set.

⊙ *Algebra* Online Question Bank

The Bonus Online Question Bank for *Algebra* consists of 25 extra practice questions (with detailed explanations) that test the variety of concepts and skills covered in this book. These questions provide you with extra practice beyond the problem sets contained in this book. You may use our online timer to practice your pacing by setting time limits for each question in the bank.

⊙ Online Updates to the Contents in this Book

The content presented in this book is updated periodically to ensure that it reflects the GMAT's most current trends. You may view all updates, including any known errors or changes, upon registering for online access.

TABLE *of* CONTENTS

guide **2**

Chapter 1

of

Algebra

PEMDAS

In This Chapter...

Subtraction of Expressions

Fraction Bars as Grouping Symbols

Chapter 1:

PEMDAS

On the GMAT, you need to know the correct order of operations when simplifying an expression. The correct order of operations is: Parentheses-Exponents-(Multiplication/Division)-(Addition/Subtraction). Multiplication and division are in parentheses because they are on the *same* level of priority. The same is true of addition and subtraction.

$$\text{Simplify } 5 + (2 \times 4 + 2)^2 - |7(-4)| + 18 \div 3 \times 5 - 8.$$

P = PARENTHESES. First, perform all the operations that are *inside* parentheses. Note that in terms of order of operations, **absolute value signs are equivalent to parentheses**. In this expression, there are two groups of parentheses:

$(2 \times 4 + 2)$ and $|7(-4)|$

In the first group, there are two operations to perform, multiplication and addition. Using PEMDAS, we see that multiplication must come before addition.

$(2 \times 4 + 2) = (8 + 2) = 10$

In the second group, there is only one operation: multiplication. We do this and then we find the absolute value.

$|7(-4)| = |-28| = 28$

Now our original expression looks like this:

$5 + 10^2 - 28 + 18 \div 3 \times 5 - 8$

E = EXPONENTS. Second, take care of any exponents in the expression. Our expression only has one exponent.

$10^2 = 100$

Now our expression looks like this:

$5 + 100 - 28 + 18 \div 3 \times 5 - 8$

M&D = <u>MULTIPLICATION & DIVISION</u>. Next, perform all the multiplication and division. It is important to note that multiplication does *not* necessarily come before division. **A group of multiplication and division operations must be performed from left to right**. The division symbol (÷) is rare on the GMAT, but you should be familiar with it nonetheless.

$$18 \div 3 \times 5$$
$$\underbrace{}$$
$$6 \quad \times \; 5 = 30$$

Now our expression reads:

$5 + 100 - 28 + 30 - 8$

A&S = <u>ADDITION & SUBTRACTION</u>. Lastly, perform all the addition and subtraction. It is important to note here again that addition does *not* necessarily come before subtraction. **A group of addition and subtraction operations must be performed from left to right**.

$5 + 100 - 28 + 30 - 8$
$105 - 28 + 30 - 8$
$77 + 30 - 8$
$107 - 8$

After performing PEMDAS, we arrive at our answer:

99

Subtraction of Expressions

One of the most common errors involving orders of operations occurs when an expression with multiple terms is subtracted. The subtraction must occur across *every* term within the expression. Each term in the subtracted part must have its sign reversed. For example:

$x - (y - z) = x - y + z$ (note that the signs of both y and $-z$ have been reversed)
$x - (y + z) = x - y - z$ (note that the signs of both y and z have been reversed)
$x - 2(y - 3z) = x - 2y + 6z$ (note that the signs of both y and $-3z$ have been reversed)

What is $5x - [y - (3x - 4y)]$?

Both expressions in parentheses must be subtracted, so the signs of each term must be reversed for *each* subtraction. Note that the square brackets are just fancy parentheses, used so that you avoid having parentheses right next to each other.

$$5x - [y - (3x - 4y)] =$$
$$5x - (y - 3x + 4y) =$$
$$5x - (5y - 3x) = 5x - 5y + 3x = \mathbf{8x - 5y}$$

Fraction Bars as Grouping Symbols

Even though fraction bars do not fit into the PEMDAS hierarchy, they do take precedence. In any expression with a fraction bar, you should **pretend that there are parentheses around the numerator and denominator of the fraction**. This may be obvious as long as the fraction bar remains in the expression, but it is easy to forget if you eliminate the fraction bar or add or subtract fractions.

Simplify: $\dfrac{x-1}{2}-\dfrac{2x-1}{3}$

The common denominator for the two fractions is 6, so multiply the numerator and denominator of the first fraction by 3, and those of the second fraction by 2:

$$\frac{x-1}{2}\left(\frac{3}{3}\right)-\frac{2x-1}{3}\left(\frac{2}{2}\right)=\frac{3x-3}{6}-\frac{4x-2}{6}$$

Treat the expressions $3x-3$ and $4x-2$ as though they were enclosed in parentheses! Accordingly, once you make the common denominator, actually put in parentheses for these numerators. Then reverse the signs of both terms in the second numerator:

$$\frac{(3x-3)-(4x-2)}{6}=\frac{3x-3-4x+2}{6}=\frac{-x-1}{6}=-\frac{x+1}{6}$$

Problem Set

1.   Evaluate: $(4 + 12 \div 3 - 18) - [-11 - (-4)]$.

2.   Evaluate: $-|-13 - (-17)|$.

3.   Evaluate: $\left(\dfrac{4+8}{2-(-6)} \right) - (4 + 8 \div 2 - (-6))$.

4.   Simplify: $x - (3 - x)$.

5.   Simplify: $(4 - y) - 2(2y - 3)$.

Solutions

P

1. **−3:** $(4 + 12 \div 3 − 18) − (−11 − (−4)) =$

$\qquad (4 + 4 − 18) − (−11 + 4) = \qquad$ division before addition/subtraction

$\qquad (−10) − (−7) = \qquad$ subtraction of negative = addition

$\qquad −10 + 7 = \text{-}3 \qquad$ arithmetic—watch the signs!

2. **−4:** $−|−13 − (−17)| =$

$\qquad −|−13 + 17| = \qquad$ subtraction of negative = addition

$\qquad −|4| = \text{-}4$

Note that the absolute value *cannot* be made into 13 + 17. You must perform the arithmetic inside grouping symbols *first*, whether inside parentheses or inside absolute-value bars. *Then* you can remove the grouping symbols.

3. $-\dfrac{25}{2}$ **or** $-12\dfrac{1}{2}$ **:** $\left[\dfrac{4 + 8}{\underbrace{2 − (−6)}} \right] − \left[4 + 8 \div 2 − (−6) \right] =$

$$\left(\dfrac{4 + 8}{\underbrace{2 + 6}} \right) − \left(4 + 8 \div 2 + 6 \right) =$$

$$\left(\dfrac{12}{8} \right) − \left(\underbrace{4 + 4 + 6} \right) =$$

$$\dfrac{3}{2} − 14 =$$

$$\dfrac{3}{2} − \dfrac{28}{2} = -\dfrac{25}{2} \text{ or } -12\dfrac{1}{2}$$

4. **$2x − 3$:** Do not forget to reverse the signs of every term in a subtracted expression.

$\qquad x − (3 − x) = x − 3 + x = 2x − 3$

5. **$−5y + 10$ (or $10 − 5y$):** Do not forget to reverse the signs of every term in a subtracted expression.

$\qquad (4 − y) − 2(2y − 3) = 4 − y − 4y + 6 = −5y + 10 \text{ (or } 10 − 5y)$

Chapter 2 of Algebra

Linear Equations

In This Chapter . . .

Chapter 2:
Linear Equations

In this chapter we will be discussing strategies related to linear equations. Linear equations are equations in which all variables have an exponent of 1. For example, the equation $x - 13 = 24$ is linear because the variable x is raised to the first power.

Before we discuss different situations that involve linear equations, we first need to discuss the difference between expressions and equations.

Expressions vs. Equations

The most basic difference between expressions and equations is that **equations contain an equals sign, and expressions do not**.

An expression, even one that contains variables, represents a value. Even if you don't know that value, **nothing you do to an expression can change its value**.

There are several methods for simplifying expressions. You can:

Combine Like Terms (ex. $6z + 5z \rightarrow 11z$)

Find a common denominator (ex. $\dfrac{1}{12} + \dfrac{3x^3}{4} \times \left(\dfrac{3}{3}\right) \rightarrow \dfrac{1}{12} + \dfrac{9x^3}{12} = \dfrac{9x^3 + 1}{12}$)

Pull out a common factor (ex. $2ab + 4b \rightarrow 2b(a + 2)$)

Cancel common factors (ex. $\dfrac{5y^3}{25y} \rightarrow \dfrac{y^2}{5}$)

What all of these moves have in common is that the value of the expression stays the same. If you plug numbers into the original and simplified forms, the value is the same. For example, replace z in the first expression with 3.

$6z + 5z$	$11z$
$6(3) + 5(3)$	$11(3)$
$18 + 15$	33
33	

2

$6z + 5z$ is equivalent to $11z$.

Equations behave differently. Equations contain an equals sign. Because it already represents an equivalence, **any change you make to one side must also be made to the other**, in order to maintain that equivalence. And while the equivalence will remain untouched, the change will alter the values on both sides of the equation.

$3 = 3$	An equivalence
$2 \times (3) = (3) \times 2$	Multiply both sides by 2
$6 = 6$	The two sides are still equal, but have different values

In general, there are 6 operations you can perform to both sides of an equation. Remember to **perform the action on the *entire* side of the equation**. For example, if you were to square both sides of the equation $\sqrt{x} + 1 = x$, you would have to square the entire expression $(\sqrt{x} + 1)$, as opposed to squaring each term individually.

You can:

Add the same thing to both sides

$$z - 13 = -14$$
$$+13 \quad +13$$
$$\overline{z \quad\quad = -1}$$

Subtract the same thing from both sides

$$x + 8 = 34$$
$$-8 \quad -8$$
$$\overline{x \quad\quad = 26}$$

Multiply both sides by the same thing

$$\frac{4}{a} = a + b$$
$$a \times \left(\frac{4}{a}\right) = (a + b) \times a$$
$$4 = a^2 + ab$$

Divide both sides by the same thing

$$3x = 6y + 12$$
$$\frac{3x}{3} = \frac{6y + 12}{3}$$
$$x = 2y + 4$$

Raise both sides to the same power

$$\sqrt{y} = y + 2$$
$$\left(\sqrt{y}\right)^2 = (y+2)^2$$
$$y = (y+2)^2$$

Take the same root of both sides

$$x^3 = 125$$
$$\sqrt[3]{x^3} = \sqrt[3]{125}$$
$$x = 5$$

2

Solving One-Variable Equations

Equations with one variable should be familiar to you from previous encounters with algebra. In order to solve one-variable equations, simply isolate the variable on one side of the equation. In doing so, make sure you perform identical operations to both sides of the equation. Here are three examples:

$3x + 5 = 26$	Subtract 5 from both sides.
$3x = 21$	Divide both sides by 3.
$x = 7$	

$w = 17w - 1$	Subtract w from both sides.
$0 = 16w - 1$	Add 1 to both sides.
$1 = 16w$	Divide both sides by 16.
$\dfrac{1}{16} = w$	

$\dfrac{p}{9} + 3 = 5$	Subtract 3 from both sides.
$\dfrac{p}{9} = 2$	Multiply both sides by 9.
$p = 18$	

Simultaneous Equations: Solving by Substitution

Sometimes the GMAT asks you to solve a system of equations with more than one variable. You might be given two equations with two variables, or perhaps three equations with three variables. In either case, there are two primary ways of solving simultaneous equations: by substitution or by combination.

Solve the following for *x* and *y*.

$$x + y = 9$$
$$2x = 5y + 4$$

2

1. Solve the first equation for x. At this point, you will not get a number, of course.

$$x + y = 9$$
$$x = 9 - y$$

2. Substitute this expression involving y into the second equation wherever x appears.

$$2x = 5y + 4$$
$$2(9 - y) = 5y + 4$$

3. Solve the second equation for y. You will now get a number for y.

$$2(9 - y) = 5y + 4$$
$$18 - 2y = 5y + 4$$
$$14 = 7y$$
$$2 = y$$

4. Substitute your solution for y into the first equation in order to solve for x.

$$x + y = 9$$
$$x + 2 = 9$$
$$x = 7$$

Simultaneous Equations: Solving by Combination

Alternatively, you can solve simultaneous equations by combination. In this method, add or subtract the two equations to eliminate one of the variables.

Solve the following for x and y.

$$x + y = 9$$
$$2x = 5y + 4$$

1. Line up the terms of the equations.

$$x + y = 9$$
$$2x - 5y = 4$$

2. The goal is to make one of two things happen: either the coefficient in front of one of the variables (say, x) is the same in both equations, in which case you subtract one equation from the other, or the coefficient in front of one of the variables is the same but with opposite signs, in which case you add the two equations. You do this by multiplying one of the equations by some number. For example, multiply the first equation by -2:

$$-2(x + y = 9) \quad \rightarrow \quad -2x - 2y = -18$$
$$2x - 5y = 4 \quad \rightarrow \quad 2x - 5y = 4$$

2

3. Add the equations to eliminate one of the variables.

$$-2x - 2y = -18$$
$$+ \quad 2x - 5y = \quad 4$$
$$\overline{\qquad -7y = -14}$$

4. Solve the resulting equation for the unknown variable.

$$-7y = -14$$
$$y = 2$$

5. Substitute into one of the original equations to solve for the second variable.

$$x + y = 9$$
$$x + 2 = 9$$
$$x = 7$$

Simultaneous Equations: Three Equations

The procedure for solving a system of three equations with three variables is exactly the same as for a system with two equations and two variables. You can use substitution or combination. This example uses both:

Solve the following for *w*, *x*, and *y*.

$$x + w = y$$
$$2y + w = 3x - 2$$
$$13 - 2w = x + y$$

1. The first equation is already solved for *y*.

$$y = x + w$$

2. Substitute for *y* in the second and third equations.

Substitute for *y* in the second equation: Substitute for *y* in the third equation:

$$2(x + w) + w = 3x - 2 \qquad\qquad 13 - 2w = x + (x + w)$$

$$2x + 2w + w = 3x - 2 \qquad\qquad 13 - 2w = 2x + w$$

$$-x + 3w = -2 \qquad\qquad\qquad 3w + 2x = 13$$

2

3. Multiply the first of the resulting two-variable equations by (−1) and combine them with addition.

$$-1(-x + 3w = -2) \quad \rightarrow \quad x - 3w = 2$$
$$3w + 2x = 13 \quad \rightarrow \quad + \quad 3w + 2x = 13$$
$$\overline{ 3x = 15}$$
$$x = 5$$

Therefore, $x = 5$

4. Use your solution for x to determine solutions for the other two variables.

$$3w + 2x = 13 \qquad\qquad y = x + w$$
$$3w + 10 = 13 \qquad\qquad y = 5 + 1$$
$$3w = 3 \qquad\qquad y = 6$$
$$w = 1$$

The preceding example requires a lot of steps to solve. Therefore, it is unlikely that the GMAT will ask you to solve such a complex system — it would be difficult to complete in two minutes. Here is the key to handling systems of three or more equations on the GMAT: look for ways to simplify the work. Look especially for shortcuts or symmetries in the form of the equations to reduce the number of steps needed to solve the system.

Take this system as an example:

What is the sum of x, y, and z?

$$x + y = 8$$
$$x + z = 11$$
$$y + z = 7$$

In this case, *do not* try to solve for x, y, and z individually. Instead, notice the symmetry of the equations — each one adds exactly two of the variables — and add them all together:

$$x + y \qquad = 8$$
$$x \qquad + z = 11$$
$$+ \qquad y + z = 7$$
$$\overline{2x + 2y + 2z = 26}$$

Therefore, $x + y + z$ is half of 26, or 13.

MANHATTAN
GMAT

Absolute Value Equations

Absolute value refers to the *positive* value of the expression within the absolute value brackets. Equations that involve absolute value generally have *two solutions*. In other words, there are *two* numbers that the variable could equal in order to make the equation true. The reason is that the value of the expression *inside* the absolute value brackets could be *positive or negative*. For instance, if you know $|x| = 5$, then x could be either 5 or −5, and the equation would still be true.

It is important to consider this rule when thinking about GMAT questions that involve absolute value. The following three-step method should be used when solving for a variable expression inside absolute value brackets. Consider this example:

> Solve for w, given that $12 + |w - 4| = 30$.

Step 1. Isolate the expression within the absolute value brackets.

$$12 + |w - 4| = 30$$
$$|w - 4| = 18$$

Step 2. Once you have an equation of the form $|x| = a$ with $a > 0$, you know that $x = \pm a$. Remove the absolute value brackets and solve the equation for 2 different cases:

CASE 1: $x = a$ (x is positive)   CASE 2: $x = -a$ (x is negative)
$$w - 4 = 18 \qquad\qquad\qquad\qquad w - 4 = -18$$
$$w = 22 \qquad\qquad\qquad\qquad\quad w = -14$$

Step 3. Check to see whether each solution is valid by putting each one back into the original equation and verifying that the two sides of the equation are in fact equal.

> In case 1, the solution, $w = 22$, is valid because $12 + |22 - 4| = 12 + 18 = 30$.
> In case 2, the solution, $w = -14$, is valid because $12 + |-14 - 4| = 12 + 18 = 30$.

Consider another example:

> Solve for n, given that $|n + 9| - 3n = 3$.

Again, isolate the expression within the absolute value brackets and consider both cases.

1. $|n + 9| = 3 + 3n$

2.   CASE 1: $n + 9$ is positive: CASE 2: $n + 9$ is negative:
$$n + 9 = 3 + 3n \qquad\qquad\qquad n + 9 = -(3 + 3n)$$
$$n = 3 \qquad\qquad\qquad\qquad\quad n = -3$$

3. The first solution, $n = 3$, is valid because $|(3) + 9| - 3(3) = 12 - 9 = 3$.

However, the second solution, $n = -3$, is *not* valid, since $|(-3) + 9| - 3(-3) = 6 + 9 = 15$. This solution fails because when $n = -3$, the absolute value expression ($n + 9 = 6$) is not negative, even though we assumed it was negative when we calculated that solution.

The possibility of a failed solution is a peculiarity of absolute value equations. For most other types of equations, it is good to check your solutions, but doing so is less critical.

Problem Set

1. Solve for x: $2(2 - 3x) - (4 + x) = 7$.

P

2. Solve for x: $x\left(x - \dfrac{5x + 6}{x}\right) = 0$.

3. Solve for z: $\dfrac{4z - 7}{3 - 2z} = -5$.

For Problems #4–8, solve for all the unknowns:

4. $\dfrac{3x - 6}{5} = x - 6$

5. $\dfrac{x + 2}{4 + x} = \dfrac{5}{9}$

6. $22 - |y + 14| = 20$

7. $y = 2x + 9$ and $7x + 3y = -51$

8. $a + b = 10$, $b + c = 12$, and $a + c = 16$

Solutions

1. **–1:** $2(2 - 3x) - (4 + x) = 7$ $-7x = 7$

    $4 - 6x - 4 - x = 7$ $x = -1$

2. **{6, –1}:** Distribute the multiplication by x. Note that, when you cancel the x in the denominator, the quantity $5x + 6$ is implicitly enclosed in parentheses!

$$x\left(x - \frac{5x + 6}{x}\right) = 0 \qquad (x - 6)(x + 1) = 0$$

$$x^2 - (5x + 6) = 0 \qquad x = 6 \text{ or } -1$$

$$x^2 - 5x - 6 = 0$$

Note also that the value 0 is impossible for x, because x is in a denominator by itself in the original equation. You are not allowed to divide by 0. Do not look at the product in the original equation and deduce that $x = 0$ is a solution.

3. **4/3:**

$$\frac{4z - 7}{3 - 2z} = -5$$

$$4z - 7 = -5(3 - 2z)$$

$$4z - 7 = -15 + 10z$$

$$8 = 6z$$

$$z = 8/6 = 4/3$$

4. **12:**

$$\frac{3x - 6}{5} = x - 6$$

$3x - 6 = 5(x - 6)$ Solve by multiplying both sides by 5 to eliminate

$3x - 6 = 5x - 30$ the denominator. Then, distribute and isolate the

$24 = 2x$ variable.

$12 = x$

5. $x = \dfrac{1}{2}$:

$$\frac{x + 2}{4 + x} = \frac{5}{9}$$

$9(x + 2) = 5(4 + x)$ Cross-multiply to eliminate the denominators.

$9x + 18 = 20 + 5x$ Then, distribute and solve.

$4x = 2$

$x = \dfrac{1}{2}$

P

6. $y = \{-16, -12\}$:

$$22 - |y + 14| = 20$$
$$|y + 14| = 2$$

First, isolate the expression within the absolute value brackets. Then, solve for two cases, one in which the expression is positive and one in which it is negative. Finally, test the validity of your solutions.

Case 1: $y + 14 = 2$ Case 2: $y + 14 = -2$
$\quad\quad\quad y = -12$ $\quad\quad\quad y = -16$

Case 1 is valid because $22 - |-12 + 14| = 22 - 2 = 20$.
Case 2 is valid because $22 - |-16 + 14| = 22 - 2 = 20$.

7. $x = -6; y = -3$:

$$y = 2x + 9 \quad\quad 7x + 3y = -51$$
$$7x + 3(2x + 9) = -51$$
$$7x + 6x + 27 = -51$$
$$13x + 27 = -51$$
$$13x = -78$$
$$x = -6$$

Solve this system by substitution. Substitute the value given for y in the first equation into the second equation. Then, distribute, combine like terms, and solve. Once you get a value for x, substitute it back into the first equation to obtain the value of y.

$$y = 2x + 9 = 2(-6) + 9 = -3$$

8. $a = 7; b = 3; c = 9$: This problem could be solved by an elaborate series of substitutions. However, because the coefficients on each variable in each equation are equal to 1, combination proves easier. Here is one way, though certainly not the only way, to solve the problem:

$$\begin{aligned} a + b \quad\quad &= 10 \\ b + c &= 12 \\ \underline{a \quad\quad + c} &= 16 \\ 2a + 2b + 2c &= 38 \end{aligned}$$

First, combine all three equations by adding them together. Then divide by 2 to get the sum of all three equations. Subtracting any of the original equations from this new equation will solve for one of the variables, and the rest can be solved by plugging back into the original equations.

$$\begin{aligned} a + b + c &= 19 \\ \underline{-(a + b \quad\quad = 10)} \\ c &= 9 \end{aligned}$$

$b + 9 = 12$ $a + 9 = 16$
$b = 3$ $a = 7$

Chapter 3

of

Algebra

Exponents

In This Chapter...

Chapter 3:

Exponents

The mathematical expression 4^3 consists of a base (4) and an exponent (3).

The expression is read as "four to the third power". The base (4) is multiplied by itself as many times as the power requires (3).

Thus, $4^3 = 4 \times 4 \times 4 = 64$.

Thus, exponents are actually shorthand for repeated multiplication.

Two exponents have special names: the exponent 2 is called the square, and the exponent 3 is called the cube.

5^2 can be read as five squared ($5^2 = 5 \times 5 = 25$).
5^3 can be read as five cubed ($5^3 = 5 \times 5 \times 5 = 125$).

All About the Base

A Variable Base

Variables can also be raised to an exponent, and behave the same as numbers.

$$y^4 = y \times y \times y \times y$$

Base of 0 or 1

0 raised to *any* power equals 0
1 raised to *any* power equals 1

For example, $0^3 = 0 \times 0 \times 0 = 0$ and $0^4 = 0 \times 0 \times 0 \times 0 = 0$.

Similarly, $1^3 = 1 \times 1 \times 1 = 1$ and $1^4 = 1 \times 1 \times 1 \times 1 = 1$.

Thus, if you are told that $x = x^2$, you know that x must be either 0 or 1.

A Fractional Base

When the base of an exponential expression is a positive proper fraction (in other words, a fraction between 0 and 1), an interesting thing occurs: as the exponent increases, the value of the expression decreases!

$$\left(\frac{3}{4}\right)^1 = \frac{3}{4} \qquad\qquad \left(\frac{3}{4}\right)^2 = \frac{3}{4} \times \frac{3}{4} = \frac{9}{16} \qquad\qquad \left(\frac{3}{4}\right)^3 = \frac{3}{4} \times \frac{3}{4} \times \frac{3}{4} = \frac{27}{64}$$

Notice that $\frac{3}{4} > \frac{9}{16} > \frac{27}{64}$. Increasing powers cause positive fractions to decrease.

You could also distribute the exponent before multiplying. For example:

$$\left(\frac{3}{4}\right)^1 = \frac{3^1}{4^1} = \frac{3}{4} \qquad\qquad \left(\frac{3}{4}\right)^2 = \frac{3^2}{4^2} = \frac{9}{16} \qquad\qquad \left(\frac{3}{4}\right)^3 = \frac{3^3}{4^3} = \frac{27}{64}$$

Note that, just like proper fractions, decimals between 0 and 1 decrease as their exponent increases:

$$(0.6)^2 = 0.36 \qquad\qquad (0.5)^4 = 0.0625 \qquad\qquad (0.1)^5 = 0.00001$$

A Compound Base

Just as an exponent can be distributed to a fraction, it can also be distributed to a product.

$$10^3 = (2 \times 5)^3 = (2)^3 \times (5)^3 = 8 \times 125 = 1{,}000$$

This also works if the base includes variables.

$$(3x)^4 = 3^4 \times x^4 = 81x^4$$

A Base of −1

$$(-1)^1 = -1 \qquad (-1)^2 = -1 \times -1 = 1 \qquad (-1)^3 = -1 \times -1 \times -1 = -1$$

This pattern repeats indefinitely. In general:

$$(-1)^{\text{ODD}} = -1 \qquad\qquad (-1)^{\text{EVEN}} = 1$$

A Negative Base

When dealing with negative bases, pay particular attention to PEMDAS. Unless the negative sign is inside parentheses, the exponent does not distribute.

$$-2^4 \qquad\qquad \neq \qquad\qquad (-2)^4$$
$$-2^4 = -1 \times 2^4 = -16 \qquad\qquad (-2)^4 = (-1)^4 \times (2)^4 = 1 \times 16 = 16$$

Any negative base will follow the same pattern as -1. Negative bases raised to an odd exponent will be negative, and any negative bases raised to an even exponent will be positive.

3

Combining Exponential Terms with Common Bases

Now that we've looked at different bases, we're going to switch our focus to the exponents themselves. The rules in this section *only* apply when the terms have the *same* base.

As you will see, all of these rules are related to the fact that exponents are shorthand for repeated multiplication.

Multiply Terms: Add Exponents

When **multiplying** two exponential terms with the same base, **add the exponents**. This rules is true no matter what the base is.

$$z^2 \times z^3 = (z \times z) \times (z \times z \times z) = z \times z \times z \times z \times z = z^5$$
$$4 \times 4^2 = (4) \times (4 \times 4) = 4 \times 4 \times 4 = 4^3$$

Fortunately, once you know the rule, you can simplify the computation greatly:

$$\left(\frac{1}{2}\right)^2 \times \left(\frac{1}{2}\right)^4 = \left(\frac{1}{2}\right)^{2+4} = \left(\frac{1}{2}\right)^6$$

Divide Terms: Subtract Exponents

When **dividing** two exponential terms with the same base, **subtract the exponents**. This rules is true no matter what the base is.

$$\frac{5^6}{5^2} = \frac{5 \times 5 \times 5 \times 5 \times \cancel{5} \times \cancel{5}}{\cancel{5} \times \cancel{5}} = 5 \times 5 \times 5 \times 5 = 5^4$$

Fortunately, once you know the rule, you can simplify the computation greatly:

$$\frac{x^{15}}{x^8} = x^{15-8} = x^7$$

Anything Raised To The Zero Equals One

This rule is an extension of the previous rule. If you divide something by itself, the quotient is 1.

$$\frac{a^3}{a^3} = \frac{\cancel{a} \times \cancel{a} \times \cancel{a}}{\cancel{a} \times \cancel{a} \times \cancel{a}} = 1$$

Look at this division by subtracting exponents.

$$\frac{a^3}{a^3} = a^{3-3} = a^0$$

Therefore, $a^0 = 1$.

A base raised to the 0 power equals 1. The one exception is a base of 0.

0^0 is *undefined*. That's because $\dfrac{0}{0}$ is undefined.

Negative Exponents

The behavior of negative exponents is also an extension of the rules for dividing exponential terms.

$$\frac{y^2}{y^5} = \frac{y \times y}{y \times y \times y \times y \times y} = \frac{1}{y^3}$$

Look at this division by subtracting exponents:

$$\frac{y^2}{y^5} = y^{2-5} = y^{-3}$$

Therefore, $y^{-3} = \dfrac{1}{y^3}$.

This is the general rule: **something with a negative exponent is just "one over" that same thing with a positive exponent.**

This rule holds true even if the negative exponent appears in the denominator, or if the negative exponent applies to a fraction.

$$\frac{1}{3^{-3}} = 3^3 \qquad\qquad \left(\frac{x}{4}\right)^{-2} = \frac{4^2}{x^2}$$

Nested Exponents: Multiply Exponents

This rule for combining terms involves raising an exponential term to an exponent. For instance, $(z^2)^3$. Expand this term to show the repeated multiplication.

$$(z^2)^3 = (z^2) \times (z^2) \times (z^2) = z^{2+2+2} = z^6$$

When you raise an exponential term to an exponent, multiply the exponents.

$$(a^5)^4 = a^{5 \times 4} = a^{20}$$

Fractional Exponents

Fractional exponents are the link between exponents and roots, which are discussed in the next chapter. Within the exponent fraction, the **numerator** tells you what **power** to raise the base to, and the **denominator** tells you which **root** to take. You can raise the base to the power and take the root in *either* order.

What is $25^{3/2}$?

The numerator of the fraction is 3, so you should raise 25 to the 3rd power. The denominator is 2, so you need to take the square root of 25^3. Note that you can rewrite 25^3 as $(5^2)^3$:

$25^{3/2} = \sqrt{25^3} = \sqrt{(5^2)^3} = 5^3 = 125$. You can also write $25^{3/2} = (5^2)^{3/2} = 5^{2 \times 3/2} = 5^3 = 125$.

Factoring Out a Common Term

Normally, exponential terms that are added or subtracted cannot be combined. However, **if two terms with the same base are added or subtracted, you can factor out a common term**.

$$11^3 + 11^4 \rightarrow 11^3(1 + 11) \rightarrow 11^3(12)$$

On the GMAT, it generally pays to factor exponential terms that have bases in common.

If $x = 4^{20} + 4^{21} + 4^{22}$, what is the largest prime factor of x?

If you want to know the prime factors of x, you need to express x as a product. Factor 4^{20} out of the expression on the right side of the equation.

$$x = 4^{20} + 4^{21} + 4^{22}$$

$$x = 4^{20}(1 + 4^1 + 4^2)$$
$$x = 4^{20}(1 + 4 + 16)$$
$$x = 4^{20}(21)$$
$$x = 4^{20}(3 \times 7)$$

Now that you have expressed x as a product, you can see that 7 is the largest prime factor of x.

Equations with Exponents

So far, we have dealt with exponential expressions. But exponents also appear in equations. In fact, the GMAT often complicates equations by including exponents or roots with unknown variables.

Here are a few situations to look out for when equations contain exponents.

Even Exponents Hide The Sign Of The Base

Any number raised to an even exponent becomes positive.

$$3^2 = 9 \quad \text{AND} \quad (-3)^2 = 9$$

Another way of saying this is that an even exponent hides the sign of its base. Compare the following two equations:

$$x^2 = 25 \qquad\qquad |x| = 5$$

Do you see what they have in common? In both cases, $x = \pm 5$. The equations share the same two solutions. In fact, there is an important relationship: **for any x, $\sqrt{x^2} = |x|$.**

Here is another example:

$a^2 - 5 = 12$ By adding 5 to both sides, you can rewrite this equation as $a^2 = 17$. This equation has two solutions: $\sqrt{17}$ and $-\sqrt{17}$.

You can also say that the equation $a^2 = 17$ has two roots. Notice that the roots or solutions of an equation do not literally have to be square roots, though!

Also note that not all equations with even exponents have 2 solutions. For example:

$x^2 + 3 = 3$ By subtracting 3 from both sides, you can rewrite this equation as $x^2 = 0$, which has only one solution: 0.

$x^2 + 9 = 0$??   Squaring can never produce a negative number! This
$x^2 = -9$??   equation does not have any solutions.

Odd Exponents Keep The Sign Of The Base

Equations that involve only odd exponents or cube roots have only 1 solution:

$x^3 = -125$ Here, x has only 1 solution: –5. You can see that (-5) $(-5)(-5) = -125$. This will not work with positive 5.

$243 = y^5$ Here, y has only 1 solution: 3. You can see that $(3)(3)$ $(3)(3)(3) = 243$. This will not work with negative 3.

3

If an equation includes some variables with odd exponents and some variables with even exponents, treat it as dangerous, as it is likely to have 2 solutions. Any even exponents in an equation make it dangerous.

Same Base or Same Exponent

In problems that involve exponential expressions on *both* sides of the equation, it is imperative to *rewrite* the bases so that either the same base or the same exponent appears on both sides of the exponential equation. Once you do this, you can usually eliminate the bases or the exponents and rewrite the remainder as an equation.

Solve the following equation for w: $(4^w)^3 = 32^{w-1}$

1. Rewrite the bases so that the same base appears on both sides of the equation. Right now, the left side has a base of 4 and the right side has a base of 32. Notice that both 4 and 32 can be expressed as powers of 2. So you can rewrite 4 as 2^2, and you can rewrite 32 as 2^5.

2. Plug the rewritten bases into the original equation.

$$(4^w)^3 = 32^{w-1}$$
$$((2^2)^w)^3 = (2^5)^{w-1}$$

3. Simplify the equation using the rules of exponents.

$$((2^2)^w)^3 = (2^5)^{w-1}$$
$$2^{6w} = 2^{5(w-1)}$$

4. Eliminate the identical bases, rewrite the exponents as an equation, and solve.

$$6w = 5w - 5$$
$$w = -5$$

You must be careful if 0, 1, or –1 is the base (or could be the base), since the outcome of raising those bases to powers is not unique. For instance, $0^2 = 0^3 = 0^{29} = 0$. So if $0^x = 0^y$, you cannot claim that

3

$x = y$. Likewise, $1^2 = 1^3 = 1^{29} = 1$, and $(-1)^2 = (-1)^4 = (-1)^{even} = 1$, while $(-1)^3 = (-1)^5 = (-1)^{odd} = -1$. Fortunately, the GMAT rarely tries to trick you this way.

Problem Set

1. $\left(\dfrac{4}{9}\right)^{-3/2}$

2. $x^3 < x^2$. Describe the possible values of x.

3. If $x^4 = 16$, what is $|x|$?

4. If $b > a > 0$, and $c \neq 0$, is $a^2 b^3 c^4$ positive?

5. Simplify: $\dfrac{m^8 p^7 r^{12}}{m^3 r^9 p} \times p^2 r^3 m^4$

6. Which of the following expressions has the largest value?

   (A) $(3^4)^{13}$ (B) $\left[(3^{30})^{12}\right]^{1/10}$ (C) $3^{30} + 3^{30} + 3^{30}$ (D) $4(3^{51})$ (E) $(3^{100})^{1/2}$

7. Simplify: $(4^y + 4^y + 4^y + 4^y)(3^y + 3^y + 3^y)$

   (A) $4^{4y} \times 3^{3y}$ (B) 12^{y+1} (C) $16^y \times 9^y$ (D) 12^y (E) $4^y \times 12^y$

8. If $4^a + 4^{a+1} = 4^{a+2} - 176$, what is the value of a?

9. If m and n are positive integers and $(2^{18})(5^m) = (20^n)$, what is the value of m?

10. Which of the following is equivalent to $\left(\dfrac{1}{3}\right)^{-4}\left(\dfrac{1}{9}\right)^{-3}\left(\dfrac{1}{27}\right)^{-2}$?

    (A) $\left(\dfrac{1}{3}\right)^{-8}$ (B) $\left(\dfrac{1}{3}\right)^{-9}$ (C) $\left(\dfrac{1}{3}\right)^{-16}$ (D) $\left(\dfrac{1}{3}\right)^{-18}$ (E) $\left(\dfrac{1}{3}\right)^{-144}$

Solutions

1. $\dfrac{27}{8}$: $\left(\dfrac{4}{9}\right)^{-3/2} = \left(\dfrac{9}{4}\right)^{3/2} = \sqrt{\left(\dfrac{9}{4}\right)^3} = \left(\sqrt{\dfrac{9}{4}}\right)^3 = \left(\dfrac{3}{2}\right)^3 = \dfrac{3^3}{2^3} = \dfrac{27}{8}$.

2. **Any non-zero number less than 1:** As positive proper fractions are multiplied, their value decreases. For example, $(1/2)^3 < (1/2)^2$. Also, any negative number will make this inequality true. A negative number cubed is negative. Any negative number squared is positive. For example, $(-3)^3 < (-3)^2$. The number zero itself, however, does not work, since $0^3 = 0^2$.

3. **2:** The possible values for x are 2 and -2. The absolute value of both 2 and -2 is 2.

4. **YES:** b and a are both positive numbers. Whether c is positive or negative, c^4 is positive. (Recall that any number raised to an even power is positive.) Therefore, the product $a^2b^3c^4$ is the product of 3 positive numbers, which will be positive.

5. $\boldsymbol{m^9p^8r^6}$: $\dfrac{m^8p^7r^{12}}{m^3r^9p} \times p^2r^3m^4 = \dfrac{m^{12}p^9r^{15}}{m^3r^9p} = m^{(12-3)}p^{(9-1)}r^{(15-9)} = m^9p^8r^6$

6. **(D):** Use the rules of exponents to simplify each expression:

   (A) $(3^4)^{13} = 3^{52}$
   (B) $\left[(3^{30})^{12}\right]^{1/10} = (3^{360})^{1/10} = 3^{360/10} = 3^{36}$
   (C) $3^{30} + 3^{30} + 3^{30} = 3(3^{30}) = 3^{31}$
   (D) $4(3^{51})$ cannot be simplified further.
   (E) $(3^{100})^{1/2} = 3^{100/2} = 3^{50}$

Answer choice (A) is clearly larger than (B), (C), and (E). You must now compare $4(3^{51})$ to 3^{52}. To make them most easily comparable, factor one 3 out of 3^{52}: $3^{52} = 3(3^{51})$. $4(3^{51})$ is greater than $3(3^{51})$, so (D) is the correct answer.

7. **(B):** $(4^y + 4^y + 4^y + 4^y)(3^y + 3^y + 3^y) = (4 \cdot 4^y)(3 \cdot 3^y) = (4^{y+1})(3^{y+1}) = (4 \cdot 3)^{y+1} = (12)^{y+1}$

8. **2:** The key to this problem is to express all of the exponential terms in terms of the greatest common factor of the terms: 4^a. Using the addition rule (or the corresponding numerical examples), you get:

$$4^a + 4^{a+1} = 4^{a+2} - 176$$
$$176 = 4^{a+2} - 4^a - 4^{a+1}$$
$$176 = 4^a \cdot (4^2) - 4^a - 4^a \cdot (4^1)$$
$$176 = 4^a \cdot (4^2 - 4^0 - 4^1)$$
$$176 = 4^a \cdot (16 - 1 - 4)$$
$$176 = 4^a \cdot (11)$$
$$4^a = 176 \div 11 = 16$$
$$a = 2$$

9. **9:** With exponential equations such as this one, the key is to recognize that as long as the exponents arc all integers, each side of the equation must have the same number of each type of prime factor. Break down each base into prime factors and set the exponents equal to each other:

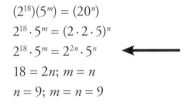

Because m and n have to be integers, there must be the **same number of 2's** on either side of the equation, and there must be the **same number of 5's** on either side of the equation. Thus $18 = 2n$ and $m = n$.

10. **(C):** Once again, you should break each base down into its prime factors first. Then, apply the negative exponent by taking the reciprocal of each term, and making the exponent positive:

$$\left(\frac{1}{3}\right)^{-4}\left(\frac{1}{9}\right)^{-3}\left(\frac{1}{27}\right)^{-2} = \left(\frac{1}{3}\right)^{-4}\left(\frac{1}{3^2}\right)^{-3}\left(\frac{1}{3^3}\right)^{-2} = 3^4 \times \left(3^2\right)^3 \times \left(3^3\right)^2 = 3^4 \times 3^6 \times 3^6 = 3^{4+6+6} = 3^{16}$$

Because all of the answer choices have negative exponents, you can perform the same transformation on them—simply take the reciprocal of each and change the exponent to a positive:

(A) $\left(\frac{1}{3}\right)^{-8} = 3^8$

(B) $\left(\frac{1}{3}\right)^{-9} = 3^9$

(C) $\left(\frac{1}{3}\right)^{-16} = \mathbf{3^{16}}$

(D) $\left(\frac{1}{3}\right)^{-18} = 3^{18}$

(E) $\left(\frac{1}{3}\right)^{-144} = 3^{144}$

MANHATTAN
GMAT

Chapter 4 of Algebra

Roots

In This Chapter...

Chapter 4:

Roots

A Square Root Has Only One Value

Compare the following two equations:

$$x^2 = 16 \qquad\qquad x = \sqrt{16}$$

Although they may seem very similar, there is an important difference. There are two solutions to the equation on the left: $x = 4$ *or* $x = -4$. There is *one* solution to the equation on the right: $x = 4$.

If an equation contains a square root on the GMAT, *only* use the positive root.

If an equation contains a squared variable, and *you* take the square root, use both the positive and the negative solutions.

This rule applies for any **even root** (square root, 4th root, 6th root, etc.). For instance:

$$\sqrt[4]{81} = 3$$

Odd roots (cube root, 5th root, 7th root, etc.) **also have only one solution.**

Odd roots, like odd exponents, keep the sign of the base.

If $\sqrt[3]{-27} = x$, what is x?

The correct answer is -3, because $(-3)(-3)(-3) = -27$.

Note that there is no solution for the even root of a negative number. No number, when multiplied an even number of times, can be negative.

Roots and Fractional Exponents

As we discussed in the previous chapter, fractional exponents are the link between roots and exponents. Within the exponent fraction, the **numerator** tells you what **power** to raise the base to, and the **denominator** tells you which **root** to take. You can raise the base to the power and take the root in *either* order.

> What is $216^{\frac{1}{3}}$?

The numerator of the fraction is 1, so you should not raise the base to any power. The denominator is 3, so you need to take the 3rd (cube) root of 216^1. In order to determine that root, you should break 216 into prime factors:

$$216 = 3 \times 3 \times 3 \times 2 \times 2 \times 2 = 6^3.$$

The 3rd root of 216 is 6, so $216^{\frac{1}{3}} = \sqrt[3]{216} = 6$.

> What is $\left(\dfrac{1}{8}\right)^{-\frac{4}{3}}$?

Because the exponent is negative, you must take the reciprocal of the base of $\left(\dfrac{1}{8}\right)$ and change the exponent to its positive equivalent. Then you must take the 3rd (cube) root to the 4th power:

$$\left(\frac{1}{8}\right)^{-\frac{4}{3}} = 8^{\frac{4}{3}} = \sqrt[3]{8^4} = \left(\sqrt[3]{8}\right)^4 = 2^4 = 16$$

You should know how to express fractional exponents in terms of roots and powers, but you should also know how to express roots as fractional exponents. The resulting expression may be much easier to simplify. Just remember that a root becomes the denominator of a fractional exponent.

> Express $\sqrt[4]{\sqrt{x}}$ as a fractional exponent.

To transform the expression into fractional exponents, you should transform the individual roots into exponents. The square root is equivalent to an exponent of $1/2$, and the fourth root is equivalent to an exponent of $1/4$. Therefore, this expression becomes $\left(x^{\frac{1}{2}}\right)^{\frac{1}{4}}$, or $x^{\frac{1}{8}}$. Note that this is equivalent to $\sqrt[8]{x}$.

Simplifying a Root

Sometimes there are two numbers inside the radical sign. In order to simplify this type of root, it is often helpful to split up the numbers into two roots and then solve. At other times, the opposite is true: you have two roots that you would like to simplify by combining them under one radical sign.

When Can You Simplify Roots?

You can only simplify roots by combining or separating them in multiplication and division. You cannot combine or separate roots in addition or subtraction.

How Can You Simplify Roots?

When multiplying roots, you can split up a larger product into its separate factors. Creating two separate radicals and simplifying each one individually before multiplying can save you from having to compute large numbers. Similarly, you can also simplify two roots that are being multiplied together into a single root of the product. For example:

$$\sqrt{25 \times 16} = \sqrt{25} \times \sqrt{16} = 5 \times 4 = 20$$
$$\sqrt{50} \times \sqrt{18} = \sqrt{50 \times 18} = \sqrt{900} = 30$$

Notice in the second example that by combining the roots first, you found a perfect square under the radical. Thus, you could simply take the square root of that number, rather than having to deal with multiple radicals in an intermediate step towards the solution.

Division of roots works the same way. You can split a larger quotient into the dividend and divisor. You can also combine two roots that are being divided into a single root of the quotient. For example:

$$\sqrt{144 \div 16} = \sqrt{144} \div \sqrt{16} = 12 \div 4 = 3$$
$$\sqrt{72} \div \sqrt{8} = \sqrt{72 \div 8} = \sqrt{9} = 3$$

The GMAT may try to trick you into splitting the sum or difference of two numbers inside a radical into two individual roots. Also, the GMAT may try to trick you into combining the sum or difference of two roots inside one radical sign. **Remember that you may only separate or combine the *product* or *quotient* of two roots. You cannot separate or combine the *sum* or *difference* of two roots.** For example:

INCORRECT: $\qquad \sqrt{16 + 9} = \sqrt{16} + \sqrt{9} = 4 + 3 = 7$

CORRECT: $\qquad \sqrt{16 + 9} = \sqrt{25} = 5$

Imperfect vs. Perfect Squares

Not all square roots yield an integer. For example: $\sqrt{52}$ does not yield an integer answer because no integer multiplied by itself will yield 52. The number 52 is an example of an imperfect square, because its square root is not an integer.

Simplifying Roots of Imperfect Squares

Some imperfect squares can be simplified into multiples of smaller square roots. For an imperfect square such as $\sqrt{52}$, you can rewrite $\sqrt{52}$ as a product of primes under the radical.

$$\sqrt{52} = \sqrt{2 \times 2 \times 13}$$

You can simplify any pairs inside the radical. In this case, there is a pair of 2's.

Since $\sqrt{2 \times 2} = \sqrt{4} = 2$, you can rewrite $\sqrt{52}$ as follows:

$$\sqrt{52} = \sqrt{2 \times 2 \times 13} = 2 \times \sqrt{13}$$

This is often written as $2\sqrt{13}$. Look at another example:

Simplify $\sqrt{72}$.

You can rewrite $\sqrt{72}$ as a product of primes: $\sqrt{72} = \sqrt{2 \times 2 \times 2 \times 3 \times 3}$. Since there are a pair of 2's and a pair of 3's inside the radical, you can simplify them.

You are left with: $\sqrt{72} = 2 \times 3 \times \sqrt{2} = 6\sqrt{2}$.

Memorize: Squares and Square Roots

You should memorize the following squares and square roots, as they often appear on the GMAT.

$1^2 = 1$	$\sqrt{1} = 1$
$1.4^2 \approx 2$	$\sqrt{2} \approx 1.4$
$1.7^2 \approx 3$	$\sqrt{3} \approx 1.7$
$2.25^2 \approx 5$	$\sqrt{5} \approx 2.25$
$2^2 = 4$	$\sqrt{4} = 2$
$3^2 = 9$	$\sqrt{9} = 3$
$4^2 = 16$	$\sqrt{16} = 4$
$5^2 = 25$	$\sqrt{25} = 5$
$6^2 = 36$	$\sqrt{36} = 6$
$7^2 = 49$	$\sqrt{49} = 7$
$8^2 = 64$	$\sqrt{64} = 8$
$9^2 = 81$	$\sqrt{81} = 9$
$10^2 = 100$	$\sqrt{100} = 10$
$11^2 = 121$	$\sqrt{121} = 11$
$12^2 = 144$	$\sqrt{144} = 12$
$13^2 = 169$	$\sqrt{169} = 13$
$14^2 = 196$	$\sqrt{196} = 14$
$15^2 = 225$	$\sqrt{225} = 15$
$16^2 = 256$	$\sqrt{256} = 16$
$20^2 = 400$	$\sqrt{400} = 20$
$25^2 = 625$	$\sqrt{625} = 25$
$30^2 = 900$	$\sqrt{900} = 30$

4

Memorize: Cubes and Cube Roots

You should memorize the following cubes and cube roots, as they often appear on the GMAT.

$1^3 = 1$	$\sqrt[3]{1} = 1$
$2^3 = 8$	$\sqrt[3]{8} = 2$
$3^3 = 27$	$\sqrt[3]{27} = 3$
$4^3 = 64$	$\sqrt[3]{64} = 4$
$5^3 = 125$	$\sqrt[3]{125} = 5$

Problem Set

1. For each of these statements, indicate whether the statement is TRUE or FALSE:

    (a) If $x^2 = 11$, then $x = \sqrt{11}$.
    (b) If $x^3 = 11$, then $x = \sqrt[3]{11}$.
    (c) If $x^4 = 16$, then $x = 2$.
    (d) If $x^5 = 32$, then $x = 2$.

Solve or simplify the following problems, using the properties of roots:

2. $\sqrt{18} \div \sqrt{2}$

3. $\sqrt{75}$

4. $\left(\dfrac{1}{81}\right)^{-\frac{1}{4}}$

5. $\sqrt{63} + \sqrt{28}$

6. $\sqrt[3]{100 - 36}$

7. $\sqrt{150} - \sqrt{96}$

8. Estimate $\sqrt{60}$.

9. $\sqrt{20a} \times \sqrt{5a}$, assuming a is positive.

10. $10\sqrt{12} \div 2\sqrt{3}$

11. $\sqrt{x^2 y^3 + 3x^2 y^3}$, assuming x and y are positive.

12. $\sqrt{0.0081}$

13. $\dfrac{\sqrt[4]{64}}{\sqrt[4]{4}}$

Solutions

1. (a) **FALSE:** Even exponents hide the sign of the original number, because they always result in a positive value. If $x^2 = 11$, then $|x| = \sqrt{11}$. Thus x could be either $\sqrt{11}$ or $-\sqrt{11}$.

(b) **TRUE:** Odd exponents preserve the sign of the original expression. Therefore, if x^3 is positive, then x must itself be positive. If $x^3 = 11$, then x must be $\sqrt[3]{11}$.

(c) **FALSE:** Even exponents hide the sign of the original number, because they always result in a positive value. If $x^4 = 16$, then x could be either 2 or -2.

(d) **TRUE:** Odd exponents preserve the sign of the original expression. Therefore, if x^5 is positive, then x must itself be positive. If $x^5 = 32$, then x must be 2.

P

2. **3:** $\sqrt{18} \div \sqrt{2} = \sqrt{9} = 3$

3. $5\sqrt{3}$ **:** $\sqrt{75} = \sqrt{25} \times \sqrt{3} = 5\sqrt{3}$

4. **3:** $\left(\dfrac{1}{81}\right)^{-\frac{1}{4}} = 81^{\frac{1}{4}} = \sqrt[4]{81} = 3$

Note: On the GMAT, when given a square root symbol with a number beneath, you are supposed to take only the positive root. This restriction does not apply when given exponents (for example, $x^2 = 16$ does give you both 4 and -4 as possible solutions).

5. $5\sqrt{7}$ **:** $\sqrt{63} + \sqrt{28} = \left(\sqrt{9} \times \sqrt{7}\right) + \left(\sqrt{4} \times \sqrt{7}\right) = 3\sqrt{7} + 2\sqrt{7} = 5\sqrt{7}$

6. **4:** $\sqrt[3]{100 - 36} = \sqrt[3]{64} = 4$

Note: Positive root restriction from above also applies here.

7. $\sqrt{6}$ **:** $\sqrt{150} - \sqrt{96} = \left(\sqrt{25} \times \sqrt{6}\right) - \left(\sqrt{16} \times \sqrt{6}\right) = 5\sqrt{6} - 4\sqrt{6} = \sqrt{6}$.

8. **7.7:** 60 is in between two perfect squares: 49, which is 7^2, and 64, which is 8^2. The difference between 64 and 49 is 15, so 60 is a little more than 2/3 of the way toward 64 from 49. A reasonable estimate for $\sqrt{60}$, then, would be about 7.7, which is a little more than 2/3 towards 8 from 7.

9. **10a:** $\sqrt{20a} \times \sqrt{5a} = \sqrt{100a^2} = 10a$

10. **10:** $10\sqrt{12} \div 2\sqrt{3} = \dfrac{10\left(\sqrt{4} \times \sqrt{3}\right)}{2\sqrt{3}} = \dfrac{20\sqrt{3}}{2\sqrt{3}} = 10$

11. $2xy\sqrt{y}$ **:** Notice that you have two terms under the radical that both contain x^2y^3. You can add like terms together if they are under the same radical: $\sqrt{x^2y^3 + 3x^2y^3} = \sqrt{(1+3)x^2y^3} = \sqrt{4x^2y^3}$.

Now, factor out all squares and isolate them under their own radical sign:

$\sqrt{4x^2 y^3} = \sqrt{4} \times \sqrt{x^2} \times \sqrt{y^2} \times \sqrt{y} = 2xy\sqrt{y}$. (Note that since x and y are positive, $\sqrt{x^2} = x$ and $\sqrt{y^2} = y$.)

12. **0.09:** Since $(0.09)(0.09) = 0.0081$, $\sqrt{0.0081} = 0.09$. You can also rewrite 0.0081 as 81×10^{-4}:

$$\sqrt{81 \times 10^{-4}} = \sqrt{81} \times \sqrt{10^{-4}} = 9 \times (10^{-4})^{1/2} = 9 \times 10^{-2} = 0.09$$

13. **2:** $\dfrac{\sqrt[4]{64}}{\sqrt[4]{4}} = \sqrt[4]{\dfrac{64}{4}} = \sqrt[4]{16} = 2$

P

Chapter 5 of Algebra

Quadratic Equations

In This Chapter...

Chapter 5:
Quadratic Equations

One special type of even exponent equation is called the quadratic equation. Here are some examples of quadratic equations:

$$x^2 + 3x + 8 = 12 \qquad w^2 - 16w + 1 = 0 \qquad 2y^2 - y + 5 = 8$$

Quadratic equations are equations with one unknown and two defining components:
- (1) a variable term raised to the second power
- (2) a variable term raised to the first power

Here are other ways of writing quadratics:

$$x^2 = 3x + 4 \qquad a = 5a^2 \qquad 6 - b = 7b^2$$

Like other even exponent equations, quadratic equations generally have 2 solutions. That is, there are usually two possible values of x (or whatever the variable is) that make the equation *true*.

Factoring Quadratic Equations

The following example illustrates the process for solving quadratic equations:

Given that $x^2 + 3x + 8 = 12$, what is x?

1. Move all the terms to the left side of the equation, combine them, and put them in the form $ax^2 + bx + c$ (where a, b, and c are integers). The right side of the equation should be set to 0. (Usually, this process makes the x^2 term positive. If not, move all the terms to the right side of the equation instead.)

$x^2 + 3x + 8 = 12$	Subtracting 12 from both sides of the equation puts all the
$x^2 + 3x - 4 = 0$	terms on the left side and sets the right side to 0.

2. Factor the equation. In order to factor, you generally need to think about two terms in the equation. Assuming that $a = 1$ (which is usually the case on GMAT quadratic equation problems), the two terms you should focus on are b and c. (If a is not equal to 1, simply divide the equation through by a.) The trick to factoring is to find two integers whose product equals c and whose sum equals b.

In the equation $x^2 + 3x - 4 = 0$, you can see that $b = 3$ and $c = -4$. In order to factor this equation, you need to find two integers whose product is -4 and whose sum is 3. The only two integers that work are 4 and -1, since you can see that $4(-1) = -4$ and $4 + (-1) = 3$.

3. Rewrite the equation in the form $(x + ?)(x + ?)$, where the question marks represent the two integers you solved for in the previous step.

$$x^2 + 3x - 4 = 0$$
$$(x + 4)(x - 1) = 0$$

4. The left side of the equation is now a product of two factors in parentheses: $(x + 4)$ and $(x - 1)$. **Since this product equals 0, one or both of the factors must be 0.**

For instance, if you know that $M \times N = 0$, then you know that either $M = 0$ or $N = 0$ (or both M and N are zero).

In this problem, set each factor in parentheses independently to 0 and solve for x.

$x + 4 = 0$ OR $x - 1 = 0$ The two solutions for x have the opposite signs
$x = -4$ $x = 1$ of the integers you found in step three.

Thus, the two solutions or roots of the quadratic equation $x^2 + 3x + 8 = 12$ are -4 and 1.

Disguised Quadratics

The GMAT will often attempt to disguise quadratic equations by putting them in forms that do not quite look like the traditional form of $ax^2 + bx + c = 0$.

Here is a very common "disguised" form for a quadratic: $3w^2 = 6w$

This is certainly a quadratic equation. However, it is very tempting to try to solve this equation without thinking of it as a quadratic. This classic mistake looks like this:

$3w^2 = 6w$ Dividing both sides by w and then dividing both sides by 3
$3w = 6$ yields the solution $w = 2$.
$w = 2$

In solving this equation without factoring it like a quadratic, we have missed one of the solutions! Let us now solve it by factoring it as a quadratic equation:

$$3w^2 = 6w$$
$$3w^2 - 6w = 0$$
$$w(3w - 6) = 0$$

Setting both factors equal to 0 yields the following solutions:

$$3w - 6 = 0$$
$$w = 0 \qquad \text{OR} \qquad 3w = 6$$
$$w = 2$$

In recognizing that $3w^2 = 6w$ is a disguised quadratic, we have found both solutions instead of accidentally missing one (in this case, the solution $w = 0$).

Here is another example of a disguised quadratic:

Solve for b, given that $\dfrac{36}{b} = b - 5$.

At first glance, this does not look like a quadratic equation, but once you begin solving the equation you should recognize that it is a quadratic.

$$\frac{36}{b} = b - 5 \qquad$$ Start by multiplying both sides of the equation by b.
After you do this, you should recognize the components of
$$36 = b^2 - 5b \qquad$$ a quadratic equation.

Now you should treat this as a quadratic equation and solve it by factoring:

$$36 = b^2 - 5b$$
$$b^2 - 5b - 36 = 0$$
$$(b - 9)(b + 4) = 0 \qquad$$ Thus, $b = 9$ or $b = -4$.

Some quadratics are hidden within more difficult equations, such as higher order equations (in which a variable is raised to the power of 3 or more). On the GMAT, these equations can almost always be factored to find the hidden quadratic expression. For example:

Solve for x, given that $x^3 + 2x^2 - 3x = 0$.

$$x^3 + 2x^2 - 3x = 0 \qquad$$ In factoring out an x from each term, you are left with the
$$x(x^2 + 2x - 3) = 0 \qquad$$ product of x and the quadratic expression $x^2 + 2x - 3$.

Now you can factor the hidden quadratic:

$$x(x^2 + 2x - 3) = 0$$
$$x(x + 3)(x - 1) = 0$$

You have a product of three factors: x, $(x + 3)$, and $(x - 1)$. This product equals 0. Thus, one of the factors equals 0.

That is, either $x = 0$ OR $x + 3 = 0$ OR $x - 1 = 0$. This equation has *three* solutions: 0, −3, and 1.

From this example, you can learn a general rule:

If you have a quadratic expression equal to 0, *and* you can factor an x out of the expression, then $x = 0$ is a solution of the equation.

Be careful not to just divide both sides by x. This division improperly eliminates the solution $x = 0$. You are only allowed to divide by a variable (or *any* expression) if you are absolutely sure that the variable or expression does not equal zero. (After all, you cannot divide by zero, even in theory.)

Taking the Square Root

So far you have seen how to solve quadratic equations by setting one side of the equation equal to zero and factoring. However, some quadratic problems can be solved without setting one side equal to zero. If the other side of the equation is a **perfect square** quadratic, the problem can be quickly solved by taking the square root of both sides of the equation.

If $(z + 3)^2 = 25$, what is z?

You could solve this problem by distributing the left-hand side of the equation, setting the right-hand side equal to zero, and factoring. However, it would be much easier to simply take the square root of both sides of the equation to solve for z. You just have to consider both the positive and the negative square root.

$$\sqrt{(z+3)^2} = \sqrt{25}$$

Note that square-rooting the square of something is the same as taking the absolute value of that thing.

$$|z + 3| = 5$$
$$z + 3 = \pm 5$$
$$z = -3 \pm 5$$
$$z = \{2, -8\}$$

Going in Reverse: Use FOIL

Instead of starting with a quadratic equation and factoring it, you may need to start with factors and rewrite them as a quadratic equation. To do this, you need to use a multiplication process called FOIL: First, Outer, Inner, Last.

MANHATTAN
GMAT

To change the expression $(x + 7)(x - 3)$ into a quadratic equation, use FOIL as follows:

First: Multiply the <u>first term</u> of each factor together: $x \times x = x^2$

Outer: Multiply the <u>outer terms</u> of the expression together: $x(-3) = -3x$

Inner: Multiply the <u>inner terms</u> of the expression together: $7(x) = 7x$

Last: Multiply the <u>last term</u> of each factor together: $7(-3) = -21$

Now, there are 4 terms: $x^2 - 3x + 7x - 21$. By combining the two middle terms, you have your quadratic expression: $x^2 + 4x - 21$.

Notice that FOIL is equivalent to distribution:
$$(x + 7)(x - 3) = x(x - 3) + 7(x - 3) = x^2 - 3x + 7x - 21.$$

If you encounter a quadratic equation, try factoring it. On the other hand, if you encounter the product of factors such as $(x + 7)(x - 3)$, you may need to use FOIL. Note: If the product of factors equals zero, then be ready to *interpret* the meaning. For instance, if you are given $(x + k)(x - m) = 0$, then you know that $x = -k$ or $x = m$.

5

Using FOIL with Square Roots

Some GMAT problems ask you to solve factored expressions that involve roots. For example, the GMAT might ask you to solve the following:

What is the value of $\left(\sqrt{8} - \sqrt{3}\right)\left(\sqrt{8} + \sqrt{3}\right)$?

Even though these problems do not involve any variables, you can solve them just like you would solve a pair of quadratic factors: use FOIL.

FIRST:	$\sqrt{8} \times \sqrt{8} = 8$	OUTER:	$\sqrt{8} \times \sqrt{3} = \sqrt{24}$
INNER:	$\sqrt{8} \times \left(-\sqrt{3}\right) = -\sqrt{24}$	LAST:	$\left(\sqrt{3}\right)\left(-\sqrt{3}\right) = -3$

The 4 terms are: $8 + \sqrt{24} - \sqrt{24} - 3$.

You can simplify this expression by removing the two middle terms (they cancel each other out) and subtracting: $8 + \sqrt{24} - \sqrt{24} - 3 = 8 - 3 = 5$. Although the problem looks complex, using FOIL reduces the entire expression to 5.

One-Solution Quadratics

Not all quadratic equations have two solutions. Some have only one solution. One-solution quadratics are also called **perfect square** quadratics, because both roots are the same. Consider the following examples:

$$x^2 + 8x + 16 = 0$$
$$(x + 4)(x + 4) = 0$$
$$(x + 4)^2 = 0 \qquad \text{Here, the only solution for } x \text{ is } -4.$$

$$x^2 - 6x + 9 = 0$$
$$(x - 3)(x - 3) = 0$$
$$(x - 3)^2 = 0 \qquad \text{Here, the only solution for } x \text{ is } 3.$$

Be careful not to assume that a quadratic equation always has two solutions. Always factor quadratic equations to determine their solutions. In doing so, you will see whether a quadratic equation has one or two solutions.

Zero In the Denominator: Undefined

Math convention does not allow division by 0. When 0 appears in the denominator of an expression, then that expression is undefined. How does this convention affect quadratic equations? Consider the following:

What are the solutions to the following equation?

$$\frac{x^2 + x - 12}{x - 2} = 0$$

We notice a quadratic equation in the numerator. Since it is a good idea to start solving quadratic equations by factoring, we will factor this numerator as follows:

$$\frac{x^2 + x - 12}{x - 2} = 0 \quad \rightarrow \quad \frac{(x - 3)(x + 4)}{x - 2} = 0$$

If either of the factors in the numerator is 0, then the entire expression becomes 0. Thus, the solutions to this equation are $x = 3$ or $x = -4$.

Note that making the denominator of the fraction equal to 0 would *not* make the entire expression equal to 0. Recall that if 0 appears in the denominator, the expression becomes undefined. Thus, $x = 2$ (which would make the denominator equal to 0) is *not* a solution to this equation. In fact, since setting x equal to 2 would make the denominator 0, the value 2 is illegal: x *cannot* equal 2.

The Three Special Products

Three quadratic expressions called *special products* come up so frequently on the GMAT that it pays to memorize them. They are GMAT favorites! You should immediately recognize these 3 expressions and know how to factor (or distribute) each one automatically. This will usually put you on the path toward the solution to the problem.

Special Product #1: $x^2 - y^2 = (x + y)(x - y)$

Special Product #2: $x^2 + 2xy + y^2 = (x + y)(x + y) = (x + y)^2$

Special Product #3: $x^2 - 2xy + y^2 = (x - y)(x - y) = (x - y)^2$

You should be able to identify these products when they are presented in disguised form. For example, $a^2 - 1$ can be factored as $(a + 1)(a - 1)$. Similarly, $(a + b)^2$ can be distributed as $a^2 + 2ab + b^2$.

Within an equation, you may need to recognize these special products in pieces. For instance, if you see $a^2 + b^2 = 9 + 2ab$, move the $2ab$ term to the left, yielding $a^2 + b^2 - 2ab = 9$. This quadratic can then be factored to $(a - b)^2 = 9$, or $a - b = \pm 3$.

Simplify: $\dfrac{x^2 + 4x + 4}{x^2 - 4}$, given that x does not equal 2 or –2.

Both the numerator and denominator of this fraction can be factored:

$$\frac{(x + 2)(x + 2)}{(x + 2)(x - 2)}$$

The expression $x + 2$ can be cancelled out from the numerator and denominator:

$$\frac{x^2 + 4x + 4}{x^2 - 4} = \frac{x + 2}{x - 2}$$

Notice that you could *not* simplify this expression if you were not told that $x \neq -2$. If $x = -2$, the expression on the left would be undefined (division by zero), whereas the expression on the right would equal 0. Thankfully, the GMAT often rules out illegal values (such as –2 in this example) that would cause division by zero.

Avoid the following common mistakes with special products:

Wrong:	Right:
$(x + y)^2 = x^2 + y^2$?	$(x + y)^2 = x^2 + 2xy + y^2$
$(x - y)^2 = x^2 - y^2$?	$(x - y)^2 = x^2 - 2xy + y^2$

Problem Set

Solve the following problems. Distribute and factor when needed:

1. If -4 is a solution for x in the equation $x^2 + kx + 8 = 0$, what is k?

2. Given that $\dfrac{d}{4} + \dfrac{8}{d} + 3 = 0$, what is d?

3. If 8 and -4 are the solutions for x, which of the following could be the equation?

    (A) $x^2 - 4x - 32 = 0$ (B) $x^2 - 4x + 32 = 0$ (C) $x^2 + 4x - 12 = 0$
    (D) $x^2 + 4x + 32 = 0$ (E) $x^2 + 4x + 12 = 0$

4. Given that $\dfrac{x^2 + 6x + 9}{x + 3} = 7$, what is x?

5. Given that $(p - 3)^2 - 5 = 0$, what is p?

6. If $x^2 + k = G$ and x is an integer, which of the following could be the value of $G - k$?

    (A) 7   (B) 8   (C) 9   (D) 10   (E) 11

7. Hugo lies on top of a building, throwing pennies straight down to the street below. The formula for the height, H, that a penny falls is $H = Vt + 5t^2$, where V is the original velocity of the penny (how fast Hugo throws it when it leaves his hand) and t is equal to the time it takes to hit the ground. The building is 60 meters high, and Hugo throws the penny down at an initial speed of 20 meters per second. How long does it take for the penny to hit the ground?

8. $\left(3 - \sqrt{7}\right)\left(3 + \sqrt{7}\right) =$

9. Given that $z^2 - 10z + 25 = 9$, what is z?

10. Data Sufficiency: What is x?

    (1) $x = 4y - 4$
    (2) $xy = 8$

Solutions

1. **6:** If -4 is a solution, then we know that $(x + 4)$ must be one of the factors of the quadratic equation. The other factor is $(x + ?)$. You know that the product of 4 and ? must be equal to 8; thus, the other factor is $(x + 2)$. You know that the sum of 4 and 2 must be equal to k. Therefore, $k = 6$.

Alternatively, if -4 is a solution, then it is a possible value for x. Plug it into the equation for x and solve for k.

$$x^2 + kx + 8 = 0$$
$$16 - 4k + 8 = 0$$
$$24 = 4k$$
$$k = 6$$

2. **{−8, −4}:** Multiply the entire equation by $4d$ (to eliminate the denominators) and factor.

$$d^2 + 32 + 12d = 0$$
$$d^2 + 12d + 32 = 0$$
$$(d + 8)(d + 4) = 0$$

$$d + 8 = 0 \qquad \text{OR} \qquad d + 4 = 0$$
$$d = -8 \qquad\qquad\qquad d = -4$$

3. **(A):** If the solutions to the equation are 8 and -4, the factored form of the equation is:
$$(x - 8)(x + 4)$$

Use FOIL to find the quadratic form: $x^2 - 4x - 32$. Therefore, the correct equation is (A).

4. **4:** Cross-multiply, simplify, and factor to solve.

$$\frac{x^2 + 6x + 9}{x + 3} = 7$$
$$x^2 + 6x + 9 = 7x + 21$$
$$x^2 - x - 12 = 0$$
$$(x + 3)(x - 4) = 0$$

$$x + 3 = 0 \qquad \text{OR} \qquad x - 4 = 0$$
$$x = -3 \qquad\qquad\qquad x = 4$$

Discard -3 as a value for x, since this value would make the denominator zero; thus, the fraction would be undefined.

5. $\{3 + \sqrt{5}, 3 - \sqrt{5}\}$:

$$(p - 3)^2 - 5 = 0$$
$$(p - 3)^2 = 5$$
$$\sqrt{(p-3)^2} = \sqrt{5}$$
$$|p - 3| = \sqrt{5}$$
$$p = 3 \pm \sqrt{5}$$

Note: If you try to distribute out $(p - 3)^2$ and solve as a quadratic, you will realize there is a non-integer solution and you can't easily solve that way. You would get:

$$p^2 - 6p + 9 - 5 = 0$$
$$p^2 - 6p + 4 = 0$$

There aren't any integers that multiply to 4 and add to 6; at this point, you could choose to use the quadratic equation to solve or you could solve using the method shown at the beginning of this explanation.

6. **(C):** $x^2 + k = G$
   $\quad\quad x^2 = G - k$

Because you know that x is an integer, x^2 is a perfect square (the square of an integer). Therefore, $G - k$ is also a perfect square. The only perfect square among the answer choices is (C) 9.

7. **2:**

$$H = Vt + 5t^2$$
$$60 = 20t + 5t^2$$
$$5t^2 + 20t - 60 = 0$$
$$5(t^2 + 4t - 12) = 0$$
$$5(t + 6)(t - 2) = 0$$

$t + 6 = 0 \quad$ OR $\quad t - 2 = 0 \qquad$ Since a time must be positive, discard the

$\quad t = -6 \qquad\qquad\quad t = 2 \qquad$ negative value for t.

8. **2:** Use FOIL to simplify this product:

F: $\quad 3 \times 3 = 9$

O: $\quad 3 \times \sqrt{7} = 3\sqrt{7}$

I: $\quad -\sqrt{7} \times 3 = -3\sqrt{7}$

L: $\quad -\sqrt{7} \times \sqrt{7} = -7$

$\quad 9 + 3\sqrt{7} - 3\sqrt{7} - 7 = 2$

Alternatively, recognize that the original expression is in the form $(x - y)(x + y)$, which is one of the three special products and which equals $x^2 - y^2$ (the difference of two squares). Thus, the expression simplifies to $3^2 - (\sqrt{7})^2 = 9 - 7 = 2$.

9. **{2, 8}:**

$$z^2 - 10z + 25 = 9$$
$$(z - 5)^2 = 9$$
$$\sqrt{(z-5)^2} = \sqrt{9}$$
$$|z - 5| = 3$$
$$z = 5 \pm 3$$

Since you recognize that the left-hand side of the equation is a perfect square quadratic, you will factor the left side of the equation first, instead of trying to set everything equal to zero.

10. **(E):** Each statement alone is not enough information to solve for x. Using statements 1 and 2 combined, if you substitute the expression for x in the first equation, into the second, you get two different answers:

$$x = 4y - 4$$
$$xy = (4y - 4)y = 8$$
$$4y^2 - 4y = 8$$
$$y^2 - y - 2 = 0$$
$$(y + 1)(y - 2) = 0$$
$$y = \{-1, 2\}$$
$$x = \{-8, 4\}$$

(E) Statements 1 and 2 TOGETHER are NOT SUFFICIENT.

P

Chapter 6

of Algebra

Formulas

In This Chapter...

Chapter 6:

Formulas

Formulas are another means by which the GMAT tests your ability to work with unknowns. Formulas are specific equations that can involve multiple variables. There are 4 major types of Formula problems which the GMAT tests:

(1)   Plug-in Formulas
(2)   Strange Symbol Formulas
(3)   Formulas with Unspecified Amounts
(4)   Sequence Formulas

The GMAT uses formulas both in abstract problems and in real-life word problems. Becoming adept at working with formulas of all kinds is critical to your GMAT success.

Plug-In Formulas

The most basic GMAT formula problems provide you with a formula and ask you to solve for one of the variables in the formula by plugging in given values for the other variables. For example:

> The formula for determining an individual's comedic aptitude, C, on a given day
> is defined as $\frac{QL}{J}$, where J represents the number of jokes told, Q represents the
> overall joke quality on a scale of 1 to 10, and L represents the number of individual
> laughs generated. If Nicole told 12 jokes, generated 18 laughs, and earned a co-
> medic aptitude of 10.5, what was the overall quality of her jokes?

Solving this problem simply involves plugging the given values into the formula in order to solve for the unknown variable Q:

$$C = \frac{QL}{J} \quad \rightarrow \quad 10.5 = \frac{18Q}{12} \quad \rightarrow \quad Q = \frac{10.5(12)}{18} \quad \rightarrow \quad Q = 7$$

The quality of Nicole's jokes was rated a 7.

Notice that you will typically have to do some rearrangement after plugging in the numbers, in order to isolate the desired unknown. The actual computations are not complex. What makes Formula problems tricky is the unfamiliarity of the given formula, which may seem to come from "out of the blue." Do not be intimidated. Simply write the equation down, plug in the numbers carefully, and solve for the required unknown.

Be sure to write the formula as a part of an equation. For instance, do not just write "$\frac{QL}{J}$" on your paper. Rather, write "$C = \frac{QL}{J}$." Look for language such as "is defined as" to identify what equals what.

Strange Symbol Formulas

Another type of GMAT formula problem involves the use of strange symbols. In these problems, the GMAT introduces an arbitrary symbol, which defines a certain procedure. These problems may look confusing because of the unfamiliar symbols. However, the symbol is *irrelevant*. All that is important is that you carefully follow each step in the procedure that the symbol indicates.

A technique that can be helpful is to break the operations down one by one and say them aloud (or in your head) — to "hear" them explicitly. Here are some examples:

FORMULA DEFINITION	STEP-BY-STEP BREAKDOWN
$x \heartsuit y = x^2 + y^2 - xy$	"The first number squared, plus the second number squared, minus the product of the two…"
$s \circ t = (s - 2)(t + 2)$	"Two less than the first number times two more than the second number…"
$\boxed{x}$ is defined as the product of all integers smaller than x but greater than 0…	"…x minus 1, times x minus 2, times x minus 3… Aha! So this is $(x - 1)$ factorial!"

Notice that it can be helpful to refer to the variables as "the first number," "the second number," and so on. In this way, you use the physical position of the numbers to keep them straight in relation to the strange symbol.

Now that you have interpreted the formula step-by-step and can understand what it means, you can calculate a solution for the formula with actual numbers. Consider the following example:

$$W \psi F = \left(\sqrt{W}\right)^F \text{ for all integers } W \text{ and } F. \text{ What is } 4 \psi 9 ?$$

The symbol ψ between two numbers signals the following procedure: take the square root of the first number and then raise that value to the power of the second number.

$$4 \ \psi \ 9 = \left(\sqrt{4}\right)^{9} = 2^{9} = 512$$

Watch out for symbols that *invert* the order of an operation. It is easy to automatically translate the function in a "left to right" manner even when that is *not* what the function specifies.

$W \ \Phi \ F = \left(\sqrt{F}\right)^{W}$ for all integers W and F. What is $4 \ \Phi \ 9$?

It would be easy in this example to mistakenly calculate the formula in the same way as the first example. However notice that the order of the operation is *reversed*—you need to take the square root of the *second* number, raised to the power of the *first* number:

$$4 \ \Phi \ 9 = \left(\sqrt{9}\right)^{4} = 3^{4} = 81.$$

More challenging strange-symbol problems require you to use the given procedure more than once. For example:

$W \ \Phi \ F = \left(\sqrt{F}\right)^{W}$ for all integers W and F. What is $4 \ \Phi \ (3 \ \Phi \ 16)$?

Always perform the procedure inside the parentheses *first*:

$$3 \ \Phi \ 16 = \left(\sqrt{16}\right)^{3} = 4^{3} = 64.$$

Now you can rewrite the original formula as follows: $4 \ \Phi \ (3 \ \Phi \ 16) = 4 \ \Phi \ 64$.

Performing the procedure a second time yields the answer:

$$4 \ \Phi \ 64 = \left(\sqrt{64}\right)^{4} = 8^{4} = 4,096.$$

Formulas with Unspecified Amounts

Some formula problems are tricky because they never give you real values; they only tell you how the value of a variable has changed.

> Cost is expressed by the formula tb^4. If b is doubled, the new cost is what percent of the original cost?
>
> (A) 200   (B) 600   (C) 800   (D) 1600   (E) 50

Notice that you do not know, nor can you know, the value of the original cost. **You need to express the new cost *in terms of* the original cost.** The only difference between the costs that you know is that b is doubled. Replace b in the original expression with $(2b)$:

Original cost = tb^4
New Cost = $t(2b)^4 \rightarrow 16tb^4$

If the original cost is tb^4, then the new cost is *sixteen times the original cost*:

$16tb^4 = 16 \times (tb^4) = 16 \times$ (original cost)

16 is equivalent to 1,600%, so the correct answer is (D).

For any formula that does not specify amounts, apply the changes the question describes directly to the original expression. You knew that b was doubled, so you doubled b $(2b)$ and plugged it right back into the original expression (tb^4).

Sequence Formulas

A sequence is a collection of numbers in a set order. Every sequence is defined by a rule, which you can use to find the values of terms.

$A_n = 9n + 3$

You can find the first term (A_1) by plugging $n = 1$ into the equation. $A_1 = 12$

You can find the second term (A_2) by plugging $n = 2$ into the equation. $A_2 = 21$

You can find the nth term (A_n) by plugging n into the equation.

If $S_n = 15n - 7$, what is the value of $S_7 - S_5$?

This question is asking for the difference of the seventh term and the fifth term of the sequence.

$S_7 = 15(7) - 7 = 105 - 7 = 98$
$S_5 = 15(5) - 7 = 75 - 7 = 68$

$S_7 - S_5 = (98) - (68) = 30$

The GMAT will expect you to recognize sequence notation. The value of the nth term is found by plugging n into the formula.

Recursive Sequences

Occasionally, a sequence will be defined *recursively*. A recursive sequence defines each term *relative* to other terms.

If $a_n = 2a_{n-1} - 4$, and $a_6 = -4$, what is the value of a_4?

If a_n represents the nth term, then a_{n-1} is the previous term. You are given the value of the 6th term, and need to figure out the value of the 4th term. You can keep track of this on your scrap paper.

$$\underline{\hspace{3cm}} \quad \underline{\hspace{3cm}} \quad \underline{\hspace{1cm}-4\hspace{1cm}}$$
$$\quad a_4 \qquad\qquad a_5 \qquad\qquad a_6$$

You can use the value of the sixth term (a_6) to find the value of the fifth term (a_5):

$$a_6 = 2a_5 - 4$$
$$(-4) = 2a_5 - 4$$
$$0 = 2a_5$$
$$0 = a_5$$

The value of the fifth term is 0.

$$\underline{\hspace{3cm}} \quad \underline{\hspace{1cm}0\hspace{1cm}} \quad \underline{\hspace{1cm}-4\hspace{1cm}}$$
$$\quad a_4 \qquad\qquad a_5 \qquad\qquad a_6$$

Now you can use the fifth term to find the fourth term:

$$a_5 = 2a_4 - 4$$
$$(0) = 2a_4 - 4$$
$$4 = 2a_4$$
$$2 = a_4$$

The value of the fourth term is 2.

When a sequence is defined recursively, the question will have to give you the value of at least one of the terms. Those values can be used to find the value of the desired term.

Sequence Problems: Alternate Method

For simple linear sequences, in which the same number is added to any term to yield the next term, you can use the following alternative method:

> If each number in a sequence is three more than the previous number, and the sixth number is 32, what is the 100th number?

Instead of finding the rule for this sequence, consider the following reasoning:

From the sixth to the one hundredth term, there are 94 "jumps" of 3. Since $94 \times 3 = 282$, there is an increase of 282 from the sixth term to the one hundredth term:

$$32 + 282 = 314.$$

Sequences and Patterns

Some sequences are easier to look at in terms of patterns, rather than rules. For example, consider the following:

> If $S_n = 3^n$, what is the units digit of S_{65}?

Clearly, you cannot be expected to multiply out 3^{65} on the GMAT. Therefore, you must assume that there is a pattern in the powers of three.

$3^1 = \mathbf{3}$
$3^2 = \mathbf{9}$
$3^3 = 2\mathbf{7}$
$3^4 = 8\mathbf{1}$
$3^5 = 24\mathbf{3}$
$3^6 = 72\mathbf{9}$
$3^7 = 2,18\mathbf{7}$
$3^8 = 6,56\mathbf{1}$

Note the pattern of the units digits in the powers of 3: 3, 9, 7, 1, [repeating]… Also note that the units digit of S_n, when n is a multiple of 4, is always equal to 1. You can use the multiples of 4 as "anchor points" in the pattern. Since 65 is 1 more than 64 (the closest multiple of 4), the units digit of S_{65} will be 3, which always follows 1 in the pattern.

As a side note, most sequences on the GMAT are defined for integer $n \geq 1$. That is, the sequence S_n almost always starts at S_1. Occasionally, a sequence might start at S_0, but in that case, you are told that $n \geq 0$. Notice that the *first* term in the sequence would then be S_0, the *second* term would be S_1, the *third* term would be S_2, and so on.

Problem Set

1. Given that $A \lozenge B = 4A - B$, what is the value of $(3 \lozenge 2) \lozenge 3$?

2. Given that 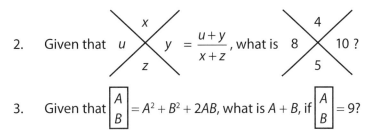 $= \dfrac{u+y}{x+z}$, what is $8 \overset{4}{\underset{5}{\times}} 10$?

3. Given that $\boxed{\begin{matrix} A \\ B \end{matrix}} = A^2 + B^2 + 2AB$, what is $A + B$, if $\boxed{\begin{matrix} A \\ B \end{matrix}} = 9$?

4. Life expectancy is defined by the formula $\dfrac{2SB}{G}$, where S = shoe size, B = average monthly electric bill in dollars, and G = GMAT score. If Melvin's GMAT score is twice his monthly electric bill, and his life expectancy is 50, what is his shoe size?

5. The "competitive edge" of a baseball team is defined by the formula $\sqrt{\dfrac{W}{L}}$, where W represents the number of the team's wins, and L represents the number of the team's losses. This year, the GMAT All-Stars had 3 times as many wins and one-half as many losses as they had last year. By what factor did their "competitive edge" increase?

For problems #6–7, use the following sequence: $A_n = 3 - 8n$.

6. What is A_1?

7. What is $A_{11} - A_9$?

8. If $a_n = \dfrac{a_{n-1} \times a_{n-2}}{2}$, $a_5 = -6$, and $a_6 = -18$, what is the value of a_3?

9. If $S_n = (4^n) + 3$, what is the units digit of S_{100}?

10. The first term in an arithmetic sequence is −5 and the second term is −3. What is the 50th term? (Recall that in an arithmetic sequence, the difference between successive terms is constant.)

Solutions

1. **37:** First, simplify $3 \lozenge 2$: $4(3) - 2 = 12 - 2 = 10$. Then, solve $10 \lozenge 3$: $4(10) - 3 = 40 - 3 = 37$.

2. **2:** Plug the numbers in the grid into the formula, matching up the number in each section with the corresponding variable in the formula $\dfrac{u+y}{x+z} = \dfrac{8+10}{4+5} = \dfrac{18}{9} = 2$.

3. **{3, –3}:**

$$A^2 + B^2 + 2AB = 9$$
$$(A + B)^2 = 9$$

$$A + B = 3 \qquad \text{OR} \qquad A + B = -3$$

First, set the formula equal to 9. Then, factor the expression $A^2 + B^2 + 2AB$. Unsquare both sides, taking both the positive and negative roots into account.

4. **Size 50:**

$$\dfrac{2SB}{2B} = 50$$
$$S = 50$$

Substitute $2B$ for G in the formula. Note that the term $2B$ appears in both the numerator and denominator, so they cancel out.

5. $\sqrt{6}$:

Let c = competitive edge

$$c = \sqrt{\dfrac{W}{L}}$$

Pick numbers to see what happens to the competitive edge when W is tripled and L is halved. If the original value of W is 4 and the original value of L is 2, the original value of c is $\sqrt{\dfrac{4}{2}} = \sqrt{2}$. If W triples to 12 and L is halved to 1, the new value of c is $\sqrt{\dfrac{12}{1}} = \sqrt{12}$. The competitive edge has increased from $\sqrt{2}$ to $\sqrt{6}$.

$$\dfrac{\sqrt{12}}{\sqrt{2}} = \sqrt{\dfrac{12}{2}} = \sqrt{6}$$

The competitive edge has increased by a factor of $\sqrt{6}$.

6. **–5:** $A_n = 3 - 8n$
$A_1 = 3 - 8(1) = 3 - 8 = -5$

7. **–16:** $A_n = 3 - 8n$
$A_{11} = 3 - 8(11) = 3 - 88 = -85$
$A_9 = 3 - 8(9) = 3 - 72 = -69$
$A_{11} - A_9 = -85 - (-69) = -16$

8. **−2:** According to the formula, $a_3 = \dfrac{a_2 \times a_1}{2}$. But you aren't given a_1 or a_2. Instead, you're given a_5 and a_6. You have to work backwards from the fifth and sixth terms of the sequence to find the third term. Notice what happens if you plug $n = 6$ into the formula:

$$a_6 = \frac{a_5 \times a_4}{2}$$

If you plug in the values of a_5 and a_6, you can solve for the value of a_4:

$$-18 = \frac{-6 \times a_4}{2}$$
$$-36 = -6 \times a_4$$
$$6 = a_4$$

Now you can use the fourth and fifth terms of the sequence to solve for a_3:

$$a_5 = \frac{a_4 \times a_3}{2}$$
$$-6 = \frac{6 \times a_3}{2}$$
$$-12 = 6 \times a_3$$
$$-2 = a_3$$

9. **9:** Begin by listing the first few terms of the sequence in order to find the pattern:

$$S_1 = 4^1 + 3 = 4 + 3 = 7$$
$$S_2 = 4^2 + 3 = 16 + 3 = 19$$
$$S_3 = 4^3 + 3 = 64 + 3 = 67$$
$$S_4 = 4^4 + 3 = 256 + 3 = 259$$

The units digit of all odd-numbered terms is 7. The units digit of all even-numbered terms is 9. Because S_{100} is an even-numbered term, its units digit will be 9.

10. **93:** The first term is −5 and the second term is −3, so you are adding +2 to each successive term. How many times do you have to add 2? There are $50 - 1 = 49$ additional "steps" after the 1st term, so you have to add +2 a total of 49 times, beginning with your starting point of −5. $-5 + 2(49) = 93$

Chapter 7 *of* Algebra

Inequalities

In This Chapter...

Chapter 6:
Inequalities

Unlike equations, which relate two equivalent quantities, inequalities compare quantities that have different values. Inequalities are used to express four kinds of relationships, illustrated by the following examples.

(1) x is less than 4

(2) x is less than or equal to 4

(3) x is greater than 4

(4) x is greater than or equal to 4

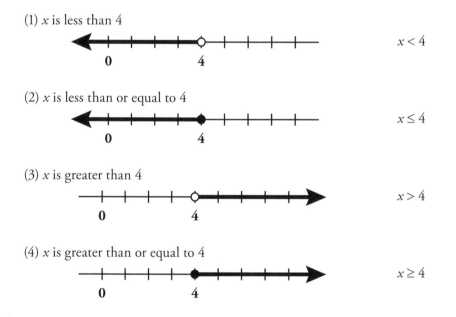

Number lines, such as those shown above, are an excellent way to visualize exactly what a given inequality means.

Much Like Equations, With One Big Exception

Many operations that can be performed on equations can be performed on inequalities. For example, in order to simplify an expression (e.g. $2 + x < 5$), you can **add or subtract a constant on both sides:**

$$2 + x < 5 \qquad\qquad x - 5 < 9$$
$$\underline{-2 \qquad -2} \qquad\qquad \underline{+5 \quad +5}$$
$$x < 3 \qquad\qquad\quad x \quad\ < 14$$

You can also **add or subtract a variable expression on both sides:**

$$y + x < 5 \qquad\qquad x - ab < 9$$
$$\underline{-y \qquad\quad -y} \qquad\qquad \underline{+\,ab \qquad +\,ab}$$
$$x < 5 - y \qquad\qquad x \qquad < 9 + ab$$

You can **multiply or divide by a *positive* number on both sides:**

$$2x < 6 \qquad\qquad 0.2x < 1$$
$$\underline{\div 2 \quad \div 2} \qquad\qquad \underline{\times 5 \qquad \times 5}$$
$$x < 3 \qquad\qquad\quad x < 5$$

There is, however, one procedure that makes inequalities different from equations: **When you multiply or divide an inequality by a negative number, the inequality sign flips!**

Given that $4 - 3x < 10$, what is the range of possible values for x?

$$4 - 3x < 10$$
$$\underline{-4 \qquad\quad -4}$$
$$-3x < 6$$
$$\underline{\div(-3) \ \div(-3)}$$
$$x > -2$$

In isolating x in this equation, you divide both sides by -3. Because you divide by a negative number, the inequality sign flips from **less than** to **greater than**!

A corollary of this is that **you cannot multiply or divide an inequality by a variable, unless you know the sign of the number that the variable stands for.** The reason is that you would not know whether to flip the inequality sign.

Combining Inequalities: Line 'Em Up!

Many GMAT inequality problems involve more than one inequality. To solve such problems, you may need to convert several inequalities to a **compound inequality**, which is a series of inequalities strung together, such as $2 < 3 < 4$. To convert multiple inequalities to a compound inequality, first line up the variables, then combine.

If $x > 8$, $x < 17$, and $x + 5 < 19$, what is the range of possible values for x?

First, solve any inequalities that need to be solved. In this example, only the last inequality needs to be solved.

$$x + 5 < 19$$
$$x < 14$$

Second, simplify the inequalities so that all the inequality symbols point in the same direction, preferably to the left (less than).

$$8 < x$$
$$x < 17$$
$$x < 14$$

Third, line up the common variables in the inequalities.

$$8 < x$$
$$x < 17$$
$$x < 14$$

$$\mathbf{8 < x < 14}$$

Notice that $x < 14$ is more limiting than $x < 17$ (in other words, whenever $x < 14$, x will always be less than 17, but not vice versa.) That is why you choose $8 < x < 14$ rather than $8 < x < 17$ as the compound inequality that solves the problem. You simply discard the less limiting inequality, $x < 17$.

Given that $u < t$, $b > r$, $f < t$, and $r > t$, is $b > u$?

Combine the 4 given inequalities by simplifying and lining up the common variables.

Simplify the list: $u < t$, $r < b$, $f < t$, and $t < r$.

Then, line up the variables…

$$u < t$$
$$r < b$$
$$f < t$$
$$t < r$$

…and combine.

$$u < t < r < b$$
$$f < t$$

When working with multiple variables, it is not always possible to combine all the inequalities, as you see in this example. You cannot really fit the inequality $f < t$ into the long combination. You do know that both u and f are less than t, but you do not know the relationship between u and f.

You can see from your combination that the answer to the question is YES: b is greater than u.

Manipulating Compound Inequalities

Sometimes a problem with compound inequalities will require you to manipulate the inequalities in order to solve the problem. You can perform operations on a compound inequality as long as you remember to perform those operations on **every term** in the inequality, not just the outside terms. For example:

$x + 3 < y < x + 5 \rightarrow x < y < x + 2$ **WRONG**: you must subtract 3 from *every* term in the inequality

$x + 3 < y < x + 5 \rightarrow x < y - 3 < x + 2$ CORRECT

$\dfrac{c}{2} \le b - 3 \le \dfrac{d}{2} \rightarrow c \le b - 3 \le d$ **WRONG**: you must multiply by 2 in *every* term in the inequality

$\dfrac{c}{2} \le b - 3 \le \dfrac{d}{2} \rightarrow c \le 2b - 6 \le d$ CORRECT

If $1 > 1 - ab > 0$, which of the following must be true?

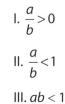

    I. $\dfrac{a}{b} > 0$

    II. $\dfrac{a}{b} < 1$

    III. $ab < 1$

(A)   I only
(B)   II only
(C)   III only
(D)   I and II only
(E)   I and III only

You can manipulate the original compound inequality as follows, making sure to perform each manipulation on every term:

$1 > 1 - ab > 0$
$0 > -ab > -1$ Subtract 1 from all three terms
$0 < ab < 1$ Multiply all three terms by −1 and flip the inequality signs

Therefore you know that $0 < ab < 1$. This tells you that ab is positive, so $\dfrac{a}{b}$ must be positive (a and b have the same sign). Therefore, I must be true. However, you do not know whether $\dfrac{a}{b} < 1$, so II is not

necessarily true. But you do know that ab must be less than 1, so III must be true. Therefore, the correct answer is (E).

Combining Inequalities: Add 'Em Up!

As discussed above, many GMAT inequality problems involve more than one inequality. Another helpful approach is to combine inequalities by **adding the inequalities together**. In order to add inequalities, you must make sure the inequality signs are facing the same direction.

> Is $a + 2b < c + 2d$?

> (1) $a < c$
> (2) $d > b$

Let's assume that you've already tried the two statements individually and neither was sufficient by itself. In order to test the statements together, you can add the inequalities together to see whether they match the question. First, you need to line up the inequalities so that they are all facing the same direction:

$$a < c$$
$$b < d$$

Then you can take the sum of the two inequalities to prove the result. You will need to add the second inequality *twice*:

$$
\begin{array}{r}
a < c \\
+\quad b < \quad d \\
\hline
a + b < c + d \\
+\quad b < \quad d \\
\hline
a + 2b < c + 2d
\end{array}
$$

If you use both statements, you can answer the question. Therefore the answer is (C).

Notice that you also could have multiplied the second inequality by 2 before summing, so that the result matched the original question:

$$
\begin{array}{r}
a < c \\
+\quad 2(b < \quad d) \\
\hline
a + 2b < c + 2d
\end{array}
$$

Adding inequalities together is a powerful technique on the GMAT. However, note that you should never subtract or divide two inequalities. Moreover, you can only multiply inequalities together under certain circumstances.

Is $mn < 10$?

    (1) $m < 2$
    (2) $n < 5$

It is tempting to multiply these two statements together and conclude that $mn < 10$. That would be a mistake, however, because both m and n could be negative numbers that yield a number larger than 10 when multiplied together. For example, if $m = -2$ and $n = -6$, then $mn = 12$, which is greater than 10.

Since you can find cases with $mn < 10$ and cases with $mn > 10$, the correct answer is (E): The two statements together are *insufficient* to answer the question definitively.

Now consider this variation:

If m and n are both positive, is $mn < 10$?

    (1) $m < 2$
    (2) $n < 5$

Since the variables are positive, you *can* multiply these inequalities together and conclude that $mn < 10$. The correct answer is (C).

Only multiply inequalities together if both sides of both inequalities are positive.

Inequalities and Absolute Value

Absolute value can be a confusing concept—particularly in a problem involving inequalities. For these types of problems, it is often helpful to try to visualize the problem with a number line.

For a simple equation such as $|x| = 5$, the graph of the solutions looks like this:

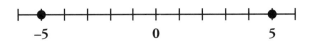

When absolute value is used in an inequality, the unknown generally has more than two possible solutions. Indeed, for a simple inequality such as $|x| < 5$, the graph of the solutions covers a range:

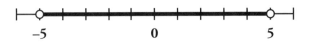

One way to understand this inequality is to say "x must be less than 5 units from zero on the number line." Indeed, **one interpretation of absolute value is simply distance on the number line**. For a simple absolute value expression such as $|x|$, we are evaluating distance from zero.

Absolute values can be more difficult to graph than the one above. Consider, for instance, the inequality $|x + 2| < 5$. This seems more difficult, because the "+ 2" term seems to throw a wrench into our distance-on-the-number-line interpretation of this problem.

However, there is a relatively straightforward way to think about this problem. First, create a number line for the term inside the absolute value bars. Here, we create a number line for "$x + 2$." We can see that this expression as a whole must be between −5 and 5:

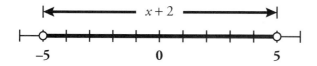

In other words, $x + 2$ must be less than 5 units away from zero on the number line. We can not stop there — we must graph for x alone. How does the "+ 2" change our graph? It forces us to shift the entire graph down by 2, because the absolute value expression will be equal to zero when $x = -2$. Thus, the graph for x alone will look like this:

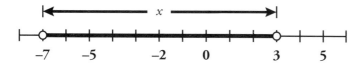

Notice that the center point for the possible values of x is now −2, which is the value for x that fits $x + 2 = 0$. This is the "center point" for the number line graph. The distance from the center point (−2) to either end point remains the same.

From this example, we can extract a standard formula for interpreting absolute value. When $|x + b| = c$, the center point of our graph is $-b$. The equation tells us that x must be *exactly* c units away from $-b$. Similarly, for the inequality $|x + b| < c$, the center point of the graph is $-b$, and the "less than" symbol tells us that x must be *less than* c units away from $-b$.

What is the graph of $|x - 4| < 3$?

Based on this formula, the center point of the graph is $-(-4) = 4$, and x must be less than 3 units away from that point:

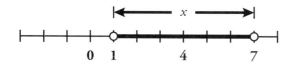

We can also solve these types of problems algebraically. Recall that equations involving absolute value require you to consider *two* scenarios: one where the expression inside the absolute value brackets is positive, and one where the expression is negative. The same is true for inequalities. For example:

Given that $|x - 2| < 5$, what is the range of possible values for x?

To work out the *first* scenario, we simply remove the absolute value brackets and solve.

$$|x - 2| < 5 \qquad\qquad x - 2 < 5 \qquad\qquad x < 7$$

To work out the *second* scenario, we reverse the signs of the terms inside the absolute value brackets, remove the brackets, and solve again.

$$
\begin{aligned}
|x - 2| &< 5 \\
-(x - 2) &< 5 \\
-x + 2 &< 5 \\
-x &< 3 \\
x &> -3
\end{aligned}
$$

We can combine these two scenarios into one range of values for x: $-3 < x < 7$. This range is illustrated by the following number line:

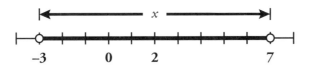

Note that this range fits in perfectly with our number-line interpretation of absolute value: this graph is the set of all points such that x is less than 5 units away from $-(-2) = 2$.

As an aside, note also that you should *never* change $|x - 5|$ to $x + 5$. This is a common mistake. Remember, when you drop the absolute value signs, you either leave the expression alone or enclose the *entire* expression in parentheses and put a negative sign in front.

Square-Rooting Inequalities

Just like equations involving even exponents, inequality problems involving even exponents require you to consider *two* scenarios. Consider this example:

If $x^2 < 4$, what are the possible values for x?

To solve this problem, recall that $\sqrt{x^2} = |x|$. For example, $\sqrt{3^2} = 3$ and $\sqrt{(-5)^2} = 5$. Therefore, when you take the square root of both sides of the inequality, you get:

$$
\begin{aligned}
\sqrt{x^2} &< \sqrt{4} \\
|x| &< 2
\end{aligned}
$$

If x is positive, then $x < 2$. On the other hand, if x is negative, then $x > -2$. Alternatively, we can just think of the problem as we did in the previous section: x must be less than 2 units away from 0 on the number line.

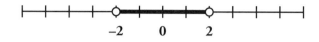

Here is another example:

If $10 + x^2 \geq 19$, what is the range of possible values for x?

$$10 + x^2 \geq 19$$
$$x^2 \geq 9$$
$$|x| \geq 3$$

If x is positive, then $x \geq 3$. If x is negative, then $x \leq -3$. Alternatively, we can just think of the problem as we did in the previous section: x must be *more than* (or exactly) 3 units away from 0 on the number line.

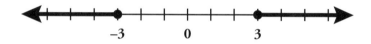

Note that you can *only* take the square root of an inequality for which both sides are definitely *not* negative, since you cannot take the square root of a negative number. Restrict this technique to situations in which the square of a variable or expression must be positive.

7

Problem Set

1. Which of the following is equivalent to $-3x + 7 \leq 2x + 32$?

    (A) $x \geq -5$ (B) $x \geq 5$ (C) $x \leq 5$ (D) $x \leq -5$

2. If $G^2 < G$, which of the following could be G?

    (A) 1   (B) $\dfrac{23}{7}$ (C) $\dfrac{7}{23}$ (D) -4 (E) -2

3. If $5B > 4B + 1$, is $B^2 > 1$?

4. If $|A| > 19$, which of the following could not be equal to A?

    (A) 26   (B) 22   (C) 18   (D) -20 (E) -24

5. If $|10y - 4| > 7$ and $y < 1$, which of the following could be y?

    (A) -0.8 (B) -0.1 (C) 0.1   (D) 0   (E) 1

6. If $a > 7$, $a + 4 > 13$, and $2a < 30$, which of the following must be true?

    (A) $9 < a < 15$ (B) $11 < a < 15$ (C) $15 < a < 20$ (D) $13 < a < 15$

7. If $d > a$ and $L < a$, which of the following cannot be true?

    (A) $d + L = 14$ (B) $d - L = 7$ (C) $d - L = 1$ (D) $a - d = 9$ (E) $a + d = 9$

8. If $\dfrac{AB}{7} > \dfrac{1}{14}$ and $A = B$, which of the following must be greater than 1?

    (A) $A + B$ (B) $1 - A$ (C) $2A^2$ (D) $A^2 - \dfrac{1}{2}$ (E) A

9. If $4x - 12 \geq x + 9$, which of the following must be true?

    (A) $x > 6$ (B) $x < 7$ (C) $x > 7$ (D) $x > 8$ (E) $x < 8$

10. If $0 < ab < ac$, is a negative?

    (1) $c < 0$
    (2) $b > c$

Solutions

1. **(A):** $-3x + 7 \leq 2x + 32$
$\qquad -5x \leq 25$
$\qquad\quad x \geq -5$

2. **(C):** IF $G^2 < G$, then G must be positive (since G^2 will never be negative), and G must be less than 1, because otherwise, $G^2 > G$. Thus, $0 < G < 1$. You can eliminate (D) and (E), since they violate the condition that G be positive. Then test (A): 1 is not less than 1, so you can eliminate (A). (B) is larger than 1, so only (C) satisfies the inequality.

3. **YES:** $\qquad 5B > 4B + 1$
$\qquad\qquad B > 1$

The squares of all numbers greater than 1 are also greater than 1. So $B^2 > 1$.

4. **(C):** If $|A| > 19$, then $A > 19$ OR $A < -19$. The only answer choice that does not satisfy either of these inequalities is (C), 18.

5. **(A):** First, eliminate any answer choices that do not satisfy the simpler of the two inequalities, $y < 1$. Based on this inequality alone, you can eliminate (E). Then, simplify the first inequality.

$$10y - 4 > 7 \qquad \text{OR} \qquad -10y + 4 > 7$$
$$10y > 11 \qquad\qquad\qquad 10y < -3$$
$$y > 1.1 \qquad\qquad\qquad\quad y < \frac{-3}{10}$$

The only answer choice that satisfies this inequality is (A) -0.8.

6. **(A):** First, solve the second and third inequalities. Simplify the inequalities, so that all the inequality symbols point in the same direction. Then, line up the inequalities as shown. Finally, combine the inequalities.

$$9 < a$$
$$\qquad a < 15 \qquad \longrightarrow \qquad 9 < a < 15$$
$$7 < a$$

Notice that all the wrong answers are more constrained: the low end is too high. The right answer will both keep out all the impossible values of a *and* let in all the possible values of a.

7. **(D):** Simplify the inequalities, so that all the inequality symbols point in the same direction. Then, line up the inequalities as shown. Finally, combine the inequalities.

$$L < a$$
$$\qquad a < d \qquad \longrightarrow \qquad L < a < d$$

Since d is a larger number than a, $a - d$ cannot be positive. Therefore, (D) cannot be true.

8. **(C):** $\dfrac{AB}{7} > \dfrac{1}{14}$

$14AB > 7$	Cross-multiply across the inequality.
$2AB > 1$	Then, divide both sides by 7.
$2A^2 > 1$	Since you know that $A = B$, $2AB = 2A^2$.

Note that we specifically tried to get the expression > 1 on the right because the question asked what must be greater than 1.

9. **(A):** $4x - 12 \geq x + 9$
$$3x \geq 21$$
$$x \geq 7$$

You were asked to pick the answer that must be true. If x is greater than or equal to 7, then x could be 7, 7.3, 8, 9.2, and so on. Which of the five answers contains an expression that covers all possible values of x? Most people will immediately look at answer (C) $x > 7$, but be careful! Does x have to be greater than 7? No; x could be 7 itself, in which case answer (C) is inaccurate. Similarly, answers (D) and (E) cover some of the possible values for x, but not *all* of them. Answer (B) doesn't share anything in common with $x > 7$, so it's wrong. You're left with answer (A). Why must it be true that x is greater than 6? Because x could be 7, 7.3, 8, 9.2 and so on. All of those possible values for x are greater than 6.

P

10. **(D):** By the transitive property of inequalities, if $0 < ab < ac$, then $0 < ac$. Therefore a and c must have the same sign. Statement (1) tells us that c is negative. Therefore, a is negative. *Sufficient.*

Statement (2) is trickier. The statement indicates that $b > c$, but the question stem also told you that $ab < ac$. When you multiply both sides of $b > c$ by a, the sign gets flipped. For inequalities, what circumstance needs to be true in order to flip the sign when you multiply by something? You multiply by a negative. Therefore, a must be negative, because multiplying the two sides of the equation by a results in a flipped inequality sign. *Sufficient.*

Chapter 8
of
Algebra

Algebra Strategies

In This Chapter...

Chapter 8:

Algebra Strategies

The following five sections appear in all 5 quant strategy guides. If you are familiar with this information, skip ahead to page 114 for new content.

Data Sufficiency Basics

Every Data Sufficiency problem has the *same* basic form:

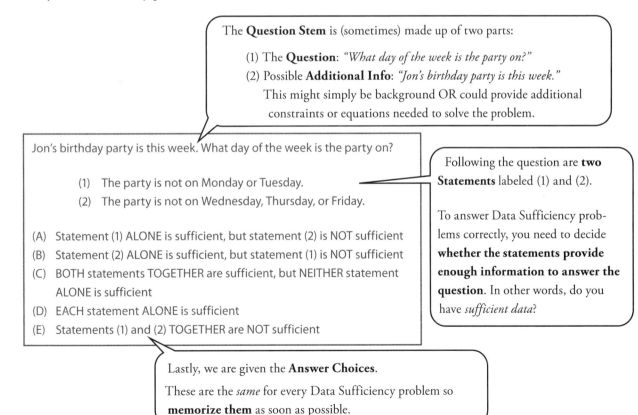

The **Question Stem** is (sometimes) made up of two parts:

(1) The **Question**: *"What day of the week is the party on?"*
(2) Possible **Additional Info**: *"Jon's birthday party is this week."*
    This might simply be background OR could provide additional constraints or equations needed to solve the problem.

Jon's birthday party is this week. What day of the week is the party on?

    (1)   The party is not on Monday or Tuesday.
    (2)   The party is not on Wednesday, Thursday, or Friday.

(A)   Statement (1) ALONE is sufficient, but statement (2) is NOT sufficient
(B)   Statement (2) ALONE is sufficient, but statement (1) is NOT sufficient
(C)   BOTH statements TOGETHER are sufficient, but NEITHER statement ALONE is sufficient
(D)   EACH statement ALONE is sufficient
(E)   Statements (1) and (2) TOGETHER are NOT sufficient

Following the question are **two Statements** labeled (1) and (2).

To answer Data Sufficiency problems correctly, you need to decide **whether the statements provide enough information to answer the question**. In other words, do you have *sufficient data*?

Lastly, we are given the **Answer Choices**.

These are the *same* for every Data Sufficiency problem so **memorize them** as soon as possible.

What Does "Sufficient" Mean?

The key to Data Sufficiency is to remember that it *does not* require you to answer the question asked in the question stem. Instead, you need to decide whether the statements provide enough information to answer the question.

Notice that in answer choices (A), (B), and (D), you are asked to evaluate each of the statements separately. You must then decide if the information given in each is sufficient (on its own) to answer the question in the stem.

The correct answer choice will be:

> **(A)** when Statement (1) provides enough information by itself, but Statement (2) does not,
> **(B)** when Statement (2) provides enough information by itself, but Statement (1) does not,
> OR
> **(D)** when BOTH statements, *independently*, provide enough information.

But what happens when you cannot answer the question with *either* statement individually? Now you must put them together and decide if all of the information given is sufficient to answer the question in the stem.

If you **must** use the statements together, the correct answer choice will be:

> **(C)** if together they provide enough information (but neither alone is sufficient),
> OR
> **(E)** if the statements, even together, do not provide enough information.

We will revisit the answer choices when we discuss a basic process for Data Sufficiency.

The DS Process

Data Sufficiency tests logical reasoning as much as it tests mathematical concepts. In order to master Data Sufficiency, develop a consistent process that will help you stay on task. It is very easy to forget what you are actually trying to accomplish as you answer these questions.

To give yourself the best chance of consistently answering DS questions correctly, you need to be methodical. The following steps can help reduce errors on every DS problem.

Step 1: Separate *additional info* from the *actual question.*

If the additional information contains *constraints* or *equations*, make a note on your scrap paper.

Step 2: Determine whether the question is Value or Yes/No.

Value: The **question** asks for the value of an unknown (e.g., What is *x*?).

> A statement is **Sufficient** when it provides **1 possible value**.
> A statement is **Not Sufficient** when it provides **more than 1 possible value**.

Yes/No: The **question** that is asked has two possible answers: Yes or No (e.g., Is *x* even?).

> A statement is **Sufficient** when it provides a **definite Yes or definite No**.
> A statement is **Not Sufficient** when the answer **could be Yes or No**.

	Sufficient	Not Sufficient
Value	**1 Value**	**More than 1 Value**
Yes/No	**1 Answer (Yes or No)**	**More than 1 Answer (Yes AND No)**

Step 3: Decide *exactly* what the question is asking.

To properly evaluate the statements, you must have a very precise understanding of the question asked in the question stem. Ask yourself two questions:

1. What, *precisely*, would be *sufficient*?
2. What, *precisely*, would *not* be *sufficient*?

For instance, suppose the question is, "What is *x*?"

1. What, precisely, would be sufficient? **One value for *x*** (e.g., *x* = 5).
2. What, precisely, would not be sufficient? **More than one value for *x*** (e.g., *x* is prime).

Step 4: Use the Grid to evaluate the statements.

The answer choices need to be evaluated in the proper order. The Grid is a simple but effective tool to help you keep track of your progress. Write the following on your page:

AD
BCE

The two columns below will tell you how to work through the Grid:

First, **evaluate Statement (1)**.

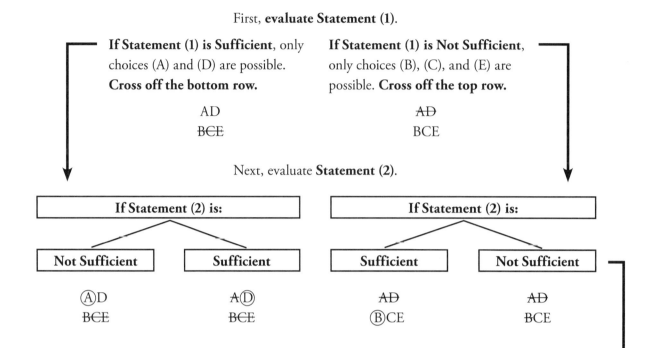

Next, evaluate **Statement (2)**.

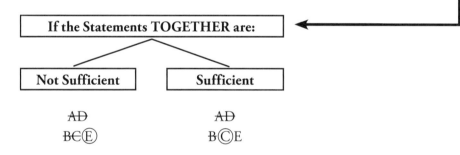

Notice that the first two steps are always the same: evaluate Statement (1) then evaluate Statement (2).

If neither Statement by itself is sufficient, then the only two possible answers are (C) and (E). The next step is to look at the Statements TOGETHER:

8

Putting It All Together

Now that you know the process, it's time to work through the practice problem start to finish.

Jon's birthday party is this week. What day of the week is the party on?

(1) The party is not on Monday or Tuesday.
(2) The party is not on Wednesday, Thursday, or Friday.

(A) Statement (1) ALONE is sufficient, but statement (2) is NOT sufficient
(B) Statement (2) ALONE is sufficient, but statement (1) is NOT sufficient
(C) BOTH statements TOGETHER are sufficient, but NEITHER statement
     ALONE is sufficient
(D) EACH statement ALONE is sufficient
(E) Statements (1) and (2) TOGETHER are NOT sufficient

Step 1: Separate *additional info* from the *actual question*.

Question	Additional Info
What day of the week is the party on?	Jon's birthday party is this week.

Step 2: Determine whether the question is Value or Yes/No.

You need to know the exact day of the week that the party is on.

This is a Value question.

Step 3: Decide *exactly* what the question is asking.

What, precisely, would be sufficient? **One possible day of the week.**
What, precisely, would not be sufficient? **More than one possible day of the week.**

Step 4: Use the Grid to evaluate the statements.

Evaluate Statement (1): Statement (1) tells you that the party is *not* on Monday or Tuesday. The party could still be on Wednesday, Thursday, Friday, Saturday, or Sunday. Statement (1) is Not Sufficient.

A̶D̶
BCE

Evaluate Statement (2): Statement (2) tells you that the party is *not* on Wednesday, Thursday, or Friday. The party could still be on Saturday, Sunday, Monday, or Tuesday. Statement (2) is Not Sufficient.

A̶D̶
B̶CE

Now that you've verified neither statement is sufficient on its own, it's time to evaluate the statements taken together.

Evaluate (1) AND (2): Taking both statements together, we know the party is not on Monday, Tuesday, Wednesday, Thursday, or Friday. The party could still be on Saturday or Sunday. Statements (1) and (2) together are Not Sufficient.

~~AD~~
~~BC~~Ⓔ

The correct answer is **(E)**.

Putting It All Together (Again)

Now try a different, but related, question:

It rains all day every Saturday and Sunday in Seattle, and never on any other day. Is it raining in Seattle right now?

(1) Today is not Monday or Tuesday.
(2) Today is not Wednesday, Thursday, or Friday.

(A) Statement (1) ALONE is sufficient, but statement (2) is NOT sufficient
(B) Statement (2) ALONE is sufficient, but statement (1) is NOT sufficient
(C) BOTH statements TOGETHER are sufficient, but NEITHER statement ALONE is sufficient
(D) EACH statement ALONE is sufficient
(E) Statements (1) and (2) TOGETHER are NOT sufficient

The statements are exactly the same as in the previous example, but the question has changed. The process is still the same.

Step 1: Separate *additional info* from the *actual question*.

Question	Additional Info
Is it raining in Seattle right now?	It rains all day every Saturday and Sunday in Seattle, and never on any other day.

Step 2: Determine whether the question is Value or Yes/No.

There are two possible answers to this question:

1.   Yes, it is raining in Seattle right now.
2.   No, it is not raining in Seattle right now.

This is a Yes/No question.

Step 3: Decide *exactly* what the question is asking.

Be careful. This part of the process is usually more complicated when the question is Yes/No. Sufficient is defined as providing a definite answer to the Yes/No question. Since the statements often allow for multiple possible values, you have to ask the Yes/No question for all the possible values.

Before you look at the statements, keep in mind there are only 7 days of the week. You know the answer to the question on each of those days as well. If today is Saturday or Sunday, the answer is **yes, it is raining in Seattle right now**. If today is Monday, Tuesday, Wednesday, Thursday, or Friday, the answer is **no, it is not raining in Seattle right now**.

What, precisely, would be sufficient? **It is definitely raining (Saturday or Sunday) OR it is definitely NOT raining (Monday through Friday).**
What, precisely, would not be sufficient? **It may be raining (e.g., Today is either Friday or Saturday).**

Step 4: Use the Grid to evaluate the statements.

Evaluate Statement (1): Statement (1) tells you that today is *not* Monday or Tuesday. Today could still be Wednesday, Thursday, Friday, Saturday, or Sunday. It might be raining in Seattle right now. You cannot know for sure. Statement (1) is Not Sufficient.

~~AD~~
BCE

Evaluate Statement (2): Statement (2) tells you that today is *not* Wednesday, Thursday, or Friday. Today could still be Saturday, Sunday, Monday, or Tuesday. It might be raining in Seattle right now. You cannot know for sure. Statement (2) is Not Sufficient.

~~AD~~
~~B~~CE

Now that you've verified neither statement is sufficient on its own, it's time to evaluate the statement taken together.

Evaluate (1) AND (2): Taking both statements together, you know that today is not Monday, Tuesday, Wednesday, Thursday, or Friday. Today could still be on Saturday or Sunday. If today is Saturday, you know that it is raining in Seattle. If today is Sunday, you know that it is raining in Seattle. Either way, you can say definitely that **yes, it is raining in Seattle right now**. Taken together, Statements (1) and (2) are Sufficient.

~~AD~~
~~B~~ⒸE

The correct answer is (**C**).

Combos

Some Data Sufficiency questions will ask for the value of a combination of variables. We call this a **Combo Problem**. Try to solve the following problem:

> What is the value of $\dfrac{x}{y}$?
>
> (1) $\dfrac{x+y}{y} = 3$
>
> (2) $y = 4$

At first glance, it may seem that you need both statements to answer the question. If you know that $y = 4$, you can use that value to solve for x in the first equation, and then find the value of x/y. This question is a **C Trap**. A C Trap appears to need both statements to answer the question. In reality, one statement by itself is enough.

Even though the question asks about 2 variables (x and y), you *don't* need to solve for x and y separately. When a question asks for a combination of variables, solve directly for the combination. In this case, you want to solve directly for x/y.

Although it may not be immediately obvious, Statement 1 by itself allows you to solve for x/y. Start by separating the numerator of the fraction $\dfrac{x+y}{y}$.

$$\frac{x+y}{y} = 3$$
$$\frac{x}{y} + \frac{y}{y} = 3$$
$$\frac{x}{y} + 1 = 3$$
$$\frac{x}{y} = 2$$

You don't know the value of x or the value of y, but you don't need to. By isolating the combination x/y, you were able to answer the question. The correct answer is (A).

When a Data Sufficiency question asks for a combination of variables, **don't try to solve for the value of each variable.** Manipulate the statements to **solve directly for the combination.**

Combos and Special Products

Try another example.

> If $x \neq y$, what is the value of $x + y$?
>
> (1) $x - y = 1$
>
> (2) $x^2 - y^2 = x - y$

The question is asking for the value of $(x + y)$. This is another combination problem. Try to solve directly for $(x + y)$.

Look at Statement 1 first. The value of $x - y$ does not tell you the value of $x + y$. If x is 4 and y is 3, $x + y$ = 7. If $x = -5$ and $y = -6$, $x + y = -11$. You can cross off answer choices (A) and (D).

Look at Statement 2. Does the expression on the left look familiar? It's one of the special products we discussed in the *Quadratic Equations* chapter. Factor $(x^2 - y^2)$:

$$x^2 - y^2 = x - y$$
$$(x + y)(x - y) = x - y$$

Now you can divide both sides by $(x - y)$:

$$\frac{(x + y)(x - y)}{(x - y)} = \frac{(x - y)}{(x - y)}$$
$$x + y = 1$$

This statement is enough by itself to give you the value of the combination $x + y$. The correct answer is (B).

As is often the case with Combo problems, one statement by itself was sufficient to answer the question.

Combos and Equations

The GMAT can make Combo problems more difficult by making them harder to spot. If a Data Sufficiency question has **an equation with multiple variables in the question stem**, it is probably a Combo in disguise. Try the following problem.

> If $a = 3bc$, what is the value of c?
>
> (1) $a = 10 - b$
> (2) $3a = 4b$

This question may ask for the value of c, but both of the statements use a and b. In this situation, **isolate the value the question asks for** (c) and **manipulate** the equation to produce the **simplest combo** you can.

$$a = 3bc$$

$$\frac{a}{3b} = c$$

$$\frac{1}{3} \times \frac{a}{b} = c$$

If you can find the value of a/b, you will have enough information to find the value of c.

Manipulate both statements to isolate a/b:

(1) $a = 10 - b$ $\rightarrow$ $\dfrac{a}{b} = \dfrac{10 - b}{b}$ INSUFFICIENT

(2) $3a = 4b$ $\rightarrow$ $\dfrac{3a}{b} = 4$ $\rightarrow$ $\dfrac{a}{b} = \dfrac{4}{3}$ SUFFICIENT

Statement 2 by itself allows us to solve for a/b.

When a Data Sufficiency question contains an equation in the question stem, **isolate the wanted variable** and create the **simplest combo** you can.

For each of the following question stems, figure out what combo the question is really asking for, and answer the Data Sufficiency question.

If $xy \neq 0$ and $\sqrt{\dfrac{xy}{3}} = x$, what is y?   If $A = \dfrac{\frac{x}{3}}{\frac{2}{y}}$, what is A ?

(1) $\dfrac{x}{y} = \dfrac{1}{3}$ (2) $x = 3$ (1) $xy = 8$ (2) $\dfrac{x}{y} = 2$

The first question asks for the value of y, so isolate y in the equation given in the question stem:

$$\sqrt{\frac{xy}{3}} = x$$

$$\frac{xy}{3} = x^2$$

$$xy = 3x^2$$

$$y = 3x$$

In other words, if you find the value of x, then you can also find the value of y. Statement 1 provides you the value of x/y, which is not enough on its own. But Statement 2 directly tells you the value of x. Statement 2 is sufficient and the correct answer is (B).

The second question asks for the value of A. A is already isolated on one side of the equation, but the right side of the equation can be simplified:

$$A = \frac{\frac{x}{3}}{\frac{2}{y}}$$

$$A = \frac{x}{3} \times \frac{y}{2}$$

$$A = \frac{xy}{6}$$

If you can find the value of xy, you will have enough information to answer the question. Statement 1 directly gives the value of xy, and is sufficient. Statement 2 gives you the value of x/y, which is not enough to find the value of xy. The correct answer is (A).

Mismatch Problems

In Combo problems, a little information can go a long way. One statement is often enough by itself to solve for a combination of variables. But sometimes even both statements put together won't be enough.

> **What is y?**
>
> (1) $x - y = 1$ (2) $xy = 12$

It is tempting to say that you have two variables, and two equations. However, when you actually combine the equations, you wind up with a quadratic equation. In the first equation, isolate x:

$$x - y = 1$$
$$x = y + 1$$

Now replace x with $(y + 1)$ in the second equation:

$$xy = 12$$
$$(y + 1)y = 12$$
$$y^2 + y = 12$$
$$y^2 + y - 12 = 0$$
$$(y + 4)(y - 3) = 0$$
$$y = -4 \text{ OR } y = 3$$

Even when the equations are combined, they do not provide enough information to find *y*, and the answer is (E).

One of the most important lessons to take away from Combos and Mismatches is this: do not make assumptions about sufficiency based on the number of variables/equations. Sometimes one statement can provide sufficient information about two variables, and sometimes two statements together are still not enough to find the value of one variable.

Inequalities and Data Sufficiency

Inequalities are a versatile tool in the hands of the GMAT. Inequalities can tell you the range of a number, the sign of a number, the relative size of two different numbers, etc.

Inequalities by their very nature force you to think about the behaviors of values as you change them.

> If *x* is an integer and $y = 2^{-x}$, is $y < \dfrac{1}{8}$?
>
> (1) $x = 4$ (2) $x > 2$

The question you need to answer is, "is $y < \dfrac{1}{8}$?" First of all, you should note that this is a Yes/No question. In fact, most Data Sufficiency questions that include inequalities are Yes/No questions.

For a statement to be sufficient, it needs to tell you definitively whether the answer is yes, *y* is less than one eighth, or no, *y* is not less than one eighth.

Let's look at Statement 1. If *x* is 4, then $y = 2^{-4}$. Notice that you can actually stop here. You have a value for *y*. You will be able to definitely answer the Yes/No question (*y* is one sixteenth, which is less than one eighth). Cross off (B), (C), and (E).

Statement 2 gives you another inequality. This inequality will only be sufficient if the answer to the Yes/No question is the same for *every possible* value of *x*.

If *x* is greater than 2, there are a large number of possible values of *x* that make *y* less than one eighth. When *x* is 5, for example, *y* equals one sixty-fourth, which is less than one eighth.

You can't try every number in a range (nor would you want to!), so you need to look for patterns that will help you figure out the best numbers to try for *x*.

Here is a pattern you can use: as *x* gets bigger, *y* gets smaller, so there is no point considering larger and larger possible *x* values. You know you can make the inequality true. The real question is, can you find a value of *x* that is small enough to make *y* greater than or equal to one eighth, to make the inequality false?

The smallest number that x is allowed to be is 3 (because x must be an integer).

$$y = 2^{-x}$$
$$y = 2^{-(3)}$$
$$y = \frac{1}{8}$$

If y can equal one eighth, then y does not have to be less than one eighth. The statement is insufficient. The correct answer is (A).

Whenever inequalities appear on Data Sufficiency, it is helpful to think about the behavior of values as you try numbers within a range. For instance, it was helpful to see that as x got larger, y got smaller. Once you found a value of x that made y less than one eighth, you didn't need to try larger values of x; you knew they would give the same result. Success on these problems requires trying to find values in a range that will give you different answers to a Yes/No question.

Testing Inequality Cases

So far we have seen several examples in which we have to consider different cases, or scenarios, for values and then determine what implications those scenarios have for the problem.

There are other common situations in which you need to consider multiple cases. Specifically, inequalities problems frequently involve testing *positive* or *negative cases* for the variables involved.

Is $d > 0$?

(1) $bc < 0$
(2) $cd > 0$

8

Clearly, Statement (1) is insufficient to answer the question, as it tells you nothing about d. Statement (2) is insufficient, because either c and d are both positive, or c and d are both negative. Therefore, you only need to test the positive/negative cases that fit Statements (1) and (2) together. That occurs when b and c have different signs, while c and d have the same sign:

b	c	d	$bc < 0$?	$cd > 0$?
+	−	−	✓	✓
−	+	+	✓	✓

It is possible that *either* b is positive and both c and d are negative, *or* b is negative and both c and d are positive. Since d could be either positive or negative, the correct answer is (E): The two statements together are *insufficient* to answer the question definitively.

Is $bd < 0$?

(1) $bc < 0$
(2) $cd > 0$

Notice that this problem is the same as the previous one, except that the question has changed. Clearly, Statement (1) is insufficient to answer the question, as it tells you nothing about d. Statement (2) is insufficient, because it tells you nothing about b. Therefore, you only need to test the positive/negative cases that fit Statements (1) and (2) together. That occurs when b and c have different signs, while c and d have the same sign:

b	c	d	$bc < 0$?	$cd > 0$?	bd?
+	−	−	✓	✓	−
−	+	+	✓	✓	−

Either way, b and d have opposite signs, so $bd < 0$. The correct answer is (C): Together the statments are *sufficient* to answer the question definitively.

Here are some common inequality statements on the GMAT, as well as what they imply. You should think of these translations whenever you see one of these statements on the test:

STATEMENT	IMPLICATION
$xy > 0$	x and y are *both positive* OR *both negative*
$xy < 0$	x and y have *different signs* (one positive, one negative)
$x^2 - x < 0$	$x^2 < x$, so $0 < x < 1$

When you see inequalities **with zero on one side of the inequality**, you should **consider using positive/negative analysis** to help solve the problem!

Fractions, Exponents, & Roots

On many GMAT problems, you need to know what happens to a fraction when you raise it to a power. The result depends on the size and sign of the fraction, as well as on the power:

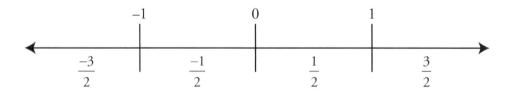

EVEN EXPONENTS (such as 2):

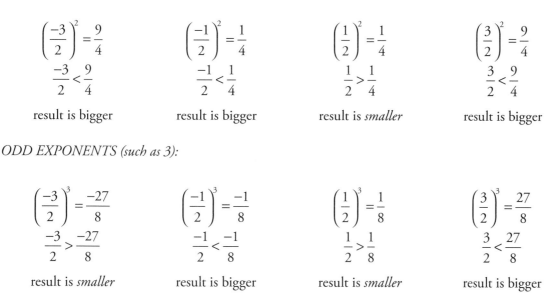

$$\left(\frac{-3}{2}\right)^2 = \frac{9}{4}$$
$$\frac{-3}{2} < \frac{9}{4}$$
result is bigger

$$\left(\frac{-1}{2}\right)^2 = \frac{1}{4}$$
$$\frac{-1}{2} < \frac{1}{4}$$
result is bigger

$$\left(\frac{1}{2}\right)^2 = \frac{1}{4}$$
$$\frac{1}{2} > \frac{1}{4}$$
result is *smaller*

$$\left(\frac{3}{2}\right)^2 = \frac{9}{4}$$
$$\frac{3}{2} < \frac{9}{4}$$
result is bigger

ODD EXPONENTS (such as 3):

$$\left(\frac{-3}{2}\right)^3 = \frac{-27}{8}$$
$$\frac{-3}{2} > \frac{-27}{8}$$
result is *smaller*

$$\left(\frac{-1}{2}\right)^3 = \frac{-1}{8}$$
$$\frac{-1}{2} < \frac{-1}{8}$$
result is bigger

$$\left(\frac{1}{2}\right)^3 = \frac{1}{8}$$
$$\frac{1}{2} > \frac{1}{8}$$
result is *smaller*

$$\left(\frac{3}{2}\right)^3 = \frac{27}{8}$$
$$\frac{3}{2} < \frac{27}{8}$$
result is bigger

As you can see, the effect of raising a fraction to a power varies depending upon the fraction's value, sign, and the exponent.

Be ready to regenerate these outcomes with test numbers such as $\frac{1}{2}$.

To raise a fraction to a negative power, simply raise the reciprocal to the equivalent positive power.

$$\left(\frac{3}{7}\right)^{-2} = \left(\frac{7}{3}\right)^2 = \frac{7^2}{3^2} = \frac{49}{9} \qquad \left(\frac{x}{y}\right)^{-w} = \left(\frac{y}{x}\right)^w = \frac{y^w}{x^w}$$

Finally, remember that taking a root of a number is the same thing as raising that number to a fractional power.

$$\sqrt{81} = (81)^{\frac{1}{2}} = 9 \qquad\qquad \sqrt[4]{x^3} = (x^3)^{\frac{1}{4}} = x^{\frac{3}{4}}$$

As a particular example, note that taking the square root of a proper fraction raises its value toward 1.

8

Replacing Variables with Numbers

Which of the following questions is easier to answer?

How many miles can a car going x miles per hour travel in y hours?

A) $\dfrac{x}{y}$ B) $\dfrac{y}{x}$ C) xy

How many miles can a car going 40 miles per hour travel in 3 hours?

A) $\dfrac{40}{3}$ B) $\dfrac{3}{40}$ C) 120

Most likely, you found the question on the right easier. In general, numbers are easier to work with than variables.

Notice that the questions are actually identical, except for the fact that x has been replaced by 40, and y has been replaced by 3. In both questions, the relevant formula is $D = RT$.

$$x \, \frac{\text{miles}}{\text{hour}} \times y \text{ hours} = xy \text{ miles}$$

$$40 \, \frac{\text{miles}}{\text{hour}} \times 3 \text{ hours} = 120 \text{ miles}$$

Problems that have **variables in the answer choices** can almost always be answered by **replacing variables with numbers**.

There are 3 basic steps.

Step 1: Identify unknowns and replace them with numbers.

In the above example, we replaced x with 40 and replaced y with 3.

Step 2: Use these numbers to calculate the answer to the problem.

A car traveling 40 miles per hour for 3 hours travels 120 miles. Remember the number you calculate in this step. We will refer to this as the target.

Step 3: Plug the same numbers into the answer choices. The correct answer will be equal to the target number.

Notice that the answer choices in the problem on the right are the same form as the answers in the problem on the left. All x's have been replaced with 40's and all y's have been replaced with 3's.

The correct answer is (C), because it equals 120, which is the same number we calculated in Step 2.

This technique can be used in questions that involve pure algebra as well.

MANHATTAN
GMAT

If $a \neq 2$, which of the following is equal to $\dfrac{b(a^2-4)}{ab-2b}$?

(A) ab (B) a (C) $a+2$ (D) a^2 (E) $2b$

Questions of this form have one goal: simplify the expression in the question stem until it looks like one of the answer choices. There are two approaches: simplify the expression, or replace the variables with numbers.

If you do not see how to simplify the expression, replacing the variables with numbers is a method that is sure to get you an answer.

In general, small primes make the best numbers to use.

Step 1: We need to pick values for a and b. Let's make $a = 3$ and $b = 5$.

Step 2: The question asks for a value equivalent to the expression $\dfrac{b(a^2-4)}{ab-2b}$. That means we need to calculate the value of this expression when $a = 3$ and $b = 5$.

$$\frac{b(a^2-4)}{ab-2b} =$$
$$\frac{(5)((3)^2-4)}{(3)(5)-2(5)} =$$
$$\frac{5(9-4)}{15-10} =$$
$$\frac{5(5)}{5} = 5$$

Our target is 5.

Step 3: Plug $a = 3$ and $b = 5$ into the answer choices and look for a match:

(A) $ab = (3)(5) = 15$
(B) $a = (3) = 3$
(C) $a + 2 = (3) + 2 = 5$
(D) $a^2 = (3)^2 = 9$
(E) $2b = 2(5) = 10$

Answer (C) matches the target, and is the correct answer.

Note that you do not necessarily have to calculate the numerical value for every single answer choice. Stop at any point when it becomes obvious that the answer cannot be the desired target answer. For example, if the target is 5 and you can tell that an answer will be negative, you can cross it off without

8

calculating the actual value. Alternatively, if you can tell the answer will be way too big or way too small for the target, you can stop and cross it off.

This technique works well for questions that ask you to simplify an expression. If you do not figure out how to simplify the expression fairly quickly, this alternative method can get you to the answer.

Note that occasionally, the numbers you pick will give you two answer choices that match the target value. For instance, in this problem, if you had picked $a = 4$ and $b = 3$, $\dfrac{b(a^2 - 4)}{ab - 2b}$ would equal 6. Answer choices (C) $(a + 2)$ and (E) $(2b)$ both equal 6 when $a = 4$ and $b = 3$.

The correct answer is correct for *any* numbers you pick. You know that (A), (B), and (D) are definitely wrong. You could then pick different numbers, calculate a new target, and retest answer choices (C) and (E).

Problem Set

Determine whether problems 1–3 are TRUE or FALSE:

1. $\left(\dfrac{-3}{4}\right)^3 > -\dfrac{3}{4}$

2. $\left(\dfrac{x+1}{x}\right)^{-2} > \dfrac{x+1}{x}$, if $x > 0$.

3. $\sqrt[4]{\left(\dfrac{3}{4}\right)^3} > \dfrac{3}{4}$

4. If $B^3A < 0$ and $A > 0$, which of the following must be negative?

   (A) AB (B) B^2A (C) B^4 (D) $\dfrac{A}{B^2}$ (E) $-\dfrac{B}{A}$

5. Given that $\dfrac{b+a}{2a} = 2$ and $a + b = 8$, what is a?

6. If $x = \dfrac{9b - 3ab}{\dfrac{3}{a} - \dfrac{a}{3}}$, what is x?

   (1) $\dfrac{9ab}{3+a} = \dfrac{18}{5}$
   (2) $b = 1$

7. Eco Wildlife Preserve contains $5x$ zebras and $2x$ lions, where x is a positive integer. If the lions succeed in killing z of the zebras, is the new ratio of zebras to lions less than 2 to 1?

   (1) $z > x$
   (2) $z = 4$

8. If $p = \dfrac{x^{a+b}}{x^b}$, what is the value of positive integer p?

   (1) $x = 5$
   (2) $a = 0$

9.   Every attendee at a monster truck rally paid the same admission fee. How many people attended the rally?

   (1)   If the admission fee had been raised to $20 and twice as many people had attended, the total admission fees collected would have been three times greater.

   (2)   If the admission fee had been raised to $30 and two-thirds as many people had attended, the total admission fees collected would have been 150% of the actual admission fees collected.

10. A retailer sells only radios and clocks. If she currently has 44 total items in inventory, how many of them are radios?

   (1)   The retailer has more than 28 radios in inventory.

   (2)   The retailer has less than twice as many radios as clocks in inventory.

P

Solutions

1. **TRUE:** Raising a proper fraction to a power causes that fraction to move closer to zero on a number line. Raising any negative number to an odd power will result in a negative number. The number $(-3/4)^3$, therefore, will be to the right of $-3/4$ on the number line.

2. **FALSE:** Any number $\dfrac{x+1}{x}$, where x is positive, will be greater than 1. Therefore, raising that number to a negative exponent will result in a number smaller than 1: $\left(\dfrac{x+1}{x}\right)^{-2} = \left(\dfrac{x}{x+1}\right)^{2} < \dfrac{x+1}{x}$ whenever x is a positive number.

3. **TRUE:** $\dfrac{3}{4}$ is a proper fraction. Any positive proper fraction raised to a power greater than 1 will result in a number smaller than the original fraction. Any positive proper fraction raised to a power between 0 and 1 will result in a number larger than the original fraction. $\sqrt[4]{\left(\dfrac{3}{4}\right)^{3}} = \left(\dfrac{3}{4}\right)^{3/4}$, which will be larger than the original fraction of $\dfrac{3}{4}$ because the exponent is between 0 and 1. $\left(\dfrac{3}{4}\right)^{3/4} \approx 0.806$. You will not have to compute the actual value of $\left(\dfrac{3}{4}\right)^{3/4}$, but you should recognize that the result is larger than $\dfrac{3}{4}$ (= 0.75).

4. **(A):** If A is positive, B^3 must be negative. Therefore, B must be negative. If A is positive and B is negative, the product AB must be negative.

5. **2:**

$$\dfrac{b+a}{2a} = 2$$
$$a+b = 8$$
$$\dfrac{1}{2a} = \dfrac{1}{4}$$

$$\dfrac{b+a}{2a(a+b)} = \dfrac{2}{8}$$
$$a = 2$$

You can divide the first equation by the second equation to solve for a quickly.

Alternatively, you could substitute for $b + a$ in the first equation, using the second.

6. **(A):** This question is really a Combos problem in disguise. Notice that the question asks for x, and the question stem contains an equation with x. You need to simplify the expression on the right side of the equation to solve for the simplest combo possible. As a general rule, simplify fractions as much as possible (eliminate them entirely if possible). Also as a general rule, if the same variable exists in more than one place in the question, attempt to combine like terms.

Begin by getting a common denominator on the bottom:

$$x = \frac{9b - 3ab}{\dfrac{3}{a} - \dfrac{a}{3}} = \frac{9b - 3ab}{\dfrac{9}{3a} - \dfrac{a^2}{3a}} = \frac{9b - 3ab}{\dfrac{9 - a^2}{3a}}$$

Now that you have only a single fraction on the bottom, you can flip it over (thus multiplying the numerator by the reciprocal of the denominator):

$$9b - 3ab \times \frac{3a}{9 - a^2} = \frac{3a(9b - 3ab)}{9 - a^2}$$

A lot of factoring can be done here! Factor common term $3b$ out of the parentheses in the numerator, and factor the denominator as the difference of squares:

$$\frac{3a(9b - 3ab)}{9 - a^2} = \frac{3a(3b)(3 - a)}{(3 - a)(3 + a)}$$

Cancel $(3 - a)$ from both top and bottom:

$$\frac{3a(3b)}{(3 + a)} = \frac{9ab}{3 + a}$$

Thus, the question is, "What is the value of $\dfrac{9ab}{3 + a}$?" You can solve the statements directly for this combo.

(1) SUFFICIENT: This statement directly gives you the value of the combo.

(2) INSUFFICIENT: Knowing the value of b does not give you the value of the combo $\dfrac{9ab}{3 + a}$.

The correct answer is (A).

7. **(A):** The ratio of zebras to lions can be written as $\dfrac{5x}{2x}$.

If z zebras then meet a sad ending, the new ratio can be written as: $\dfrac{5x - z}{2x}$.

(Note, it's fine to "mix" the ratio with the variable z, since the ratio itself already contains the variable x, which is the multiplier — that is, x is the number you would multiply 5 and 2 by to get the real, original numbers of zebras and lions.)

Thus, you can rephrase the question as:

$$\frac{5x - z}{2x} < \frac{2}{1}?$$

But you can keep simplifying! (If the DS question contains fractions, or the same variable in more than one place, try to simplify a bit more.) Since you know that x is positive, you can cross-multiply:

$$5x - z < 4x?$$
$$-z < -x?$$
$$z > x?$$

The question is asking, "Is $z > x$?"

(1) SUFFICIENT: This statement answers the rephrased question directly.

Alternately, plugging in values for z and x would also show the statement to be sufficient. For instance, if $z = 3$ and $x = 2$, then you would start with 10 zebras and 4 lions, and then losing three zebras would give you 7 zebras to 4 lions, which is less than a 2 to 1 ratio. Additional examples will yield the same results.

(2) INSUFFICIENT: Knowing that $z = 4$ is not sufficient without knowing something about x. For instance, if $x = 1$ and you began with 5 zebras and 2 lions, then losing 4 zebras would certainly shift the ratio below 2 to 1. But what if x were 100? If you began with 500 zebras and 200 lions, then the loss of 4 zebras would not shift the ratio below 2 to 1.

The correct answer is (A).

8. **(B):** This question isn't really about p. It's about the expression $\dfrac{x^{a+b}}{x^{b}}$, which can be simplified by subtracting the exponent in the denominator from the exponent in the numerator:

$$\frac{x^{a+b}}{x^{b}} = x^{a+b-(b)} = x^{a}$$

So our question may be rephrased as simply, what is x^{a}?

Be careful, though—sufficiency in this case does *not* necessarily mean that you need to know x and a individually. (As just one example, if x is 1, then a is not needed, because 1 to any power is still 1).

(1) INSUFFICIENT: Knowing that x is 5 is not sufficient without knowing a.

(2) SUFFICIENT: Anything to the 0 power is 1. The only exception to the rule is 0. 0^{0} is undefined. However, you have been told that p is a positive integer, so you know that x cannot equal 0.

The correct answer is (B).

MANHATTAN
GMAT

9. **(E):** This question asks how many people attended a monster truck rally. The number of attendees times the admission fee equals the total amount collected, as such:

Total = Attendees × Price
$T = A \times P$

You want to know A.

(1) INSUFFICIENT: If the price had been $20 and twice as many people had attended, the total would be three times greater. Therefore:

$3T = 2A \times 20$
$3T = 40A$

This is not sufficient to solve for A.

(2) INSUFFICIENT: If the price had been $30 and two-thirds as many people had attended, the total would be 150% of the actual total. Therefore:

$$1.5T = \frac{2}{3}A \times 30$$
$$1.5T = 20A$$

This is not sufficient to solve for A.

(1) AND (2) INSUFFICIENT: Don't fall for the trap that two equations for two variables is enough to solve. Notice that $3T = 40A$ and $1.5T = 20A$ are identical. Combining the two statements is therefore no more sufficient than either statement alone.

The correct answer is (E).

10. **(C):** First assign r = the number of radios the retailer has in inventory and c = the number of clocks the retailer has in inventory. You can translate the information in the question stem:

$r + c = 44$

The question now becomes: What is r?

(1) INSUFFICIENT: This only tells you that $r \geq 29$. r could equal 29, 30, 40, etc.

(2) INSUFFICIENT: This only tells you that $r < 2c$. Combining this information with the original equation from the problem gives you:

$r < 2c$
$r + c = 44$

If you isolate c in the second equation, you can then substitute into the inequality:

$c = 44 - r$

$r < 2c$
$r < 2(44 - r)$
$r < 88 - 2r$
$3r < 88$
$r < \dfrac{88}{3}$

88/3 is equal to 29 $\frac{1}{3}$. Therefore, you know that r must be less than or equal to 29 (because r must be an integer). This information on its own, however, is insufficient.

(1) AND (2) SUFFICIENT: Statement 1 tells you $r \geq 29$ and Statement 2 tells you $r \leq 29$. r must equal 29.

The correct answer is (C).

P

Chapter 9
of Algebra

Extra Equations Strategies

In This Chapter. . .

Chapter 9:
Extra Equations Strategies

Complex Absolute Value Equations

So far we have only looked at absolute value equations that have one unknown inside one absolute value expression. However, these equations can get more complicated by including more than one absolute value expression. There are two primary types of these *complex* absolute value equations:

(1) The equation contains *two* or more variables in more than one absolute value expression. These equations, which usually lack constants, are generally *not* easy to solve with algebra. Instead, a conceptual approach is preferable. Problems of this type are discussed in the "Positives & Negatives Strategy" chapter of the Manhattan GMAT *Number Properties* Strategy Guide.

(2) The equation contains *one* variable and at least one *constant* in more than one absolute value expression. These equations are usually easier to solve with an algebraic approach than with a conceptual approach. For example:

If $|x - 2| = |2x - 3|$, what are the possible values for *x*?

We have one variable (*x*) and three constants (−2, 2 and −3). Thus we know that we should take an algebraic approach to the problem.

Because there are two absolute value expressions, each of which yields two algebraic cases, it seems that we need to test *four* cases overall: positive/positive, positive/negative, negative/positive, and negative/negative.

(1) The positive/positive case:	$(x - 2) = (2x - 3)$
(2) The positive/negative case:	$(x - 2) = -(2x - 3)$
(3) The negative/positive case:	$-(x - 2) = (2x - 3)$
(4) The negative/negative case:	$-(x - 2) = -(2x - 3)$

However, note that case (1) and case (4) yield the same equation. Likewise, case (2) and case (3) yield the same equation. Thus, you only need to consider two real cases: one in which neither expression changes sign, and another in which one expression changes sign.

CASE A: Same sign   CASE B: Different signs

$(x - 2) = (2x - 3)$ $(x - 2) = -(2x - 3)$

$1 = x$ $3x = 5$

$x = 5/3$

You also have to check the validity of the solutions once you have solved the equations.

Both solutions are valid, because $|1 - 2| = |2(1) - 3| = 1$, and $\left|\dfrac{5}{3} - 2\right| = \left|2\left(\dfrac{5}{3}\right) - 3\right| = \dfrac{1}{3}$.

Integer Constraints

Occasionally, a GMAT algebra problem contains integer constraints. In such a case, there might be many possible solutions among all numbers but only one *integer* solution.

$2y - x = 2xy$ and $x \ne 0$. If x and y are integers, which of the following could equal y?

    (A)   2
    (B)   1
    (C)   0
    (D) −1
    (E) −2

First, solve for x in terms of y, so that you can test values of y in the answer choices.

$$2y - x = 2xy \qquad 2y = 2xy + x \qquad 2y = x(2y + 1) \qquad x = \dfrac{2y}{2y+1}$$

Ordinarily, this result would not be enough for you to reach an answer. However, you know that both x and y must be integers. Therefore, you should find which integer value of y generates an integer value for x.

Now, test the possibilities for y, using the answer choices. The case $y = 0$ produces $x = 0$, but this outcome is disallowed by the condition that $x \ne 0$. The only other case that produces an integer value for x is $y = -1$, yielding $x = 2$. Thus, the answer is **(D)**. Integer constraints together with *inequalities* can also lead to just one solution.

If x and y are nonnegative integers and $x + y = 25$, what is x?

    (1) $20x + 10y < 300$
    (2) $20x + 10y > 280$

First, you should note that since x and y must be positive integers, the smallest possible value for $20x + 10y$ is 250, when $x = 0$ and $y = 25$. Statement (1) does not tell you what x is, nor does statement (2). However, if you combine the statements, you get:

Substituting $(25 - x)$ for y:

$$280 < 20x + 10y < 300$$
$$280 < 20x + 10(25 - x) < 300$$
$$280 < 20x + 250 - 10x < 300$$
$$30 < 10x < 50$$
$$3 < x < 5$$

Since x must be an integer, x must equal 4. Therefore the answer is **(C)**: Statements 1 and 2 TOGETHER are sufficient. (Incidentally, if you relax the integer constraint, x can be any real number that is more than 3 and less than 5.)

Multiplying or Dividing Two Equations

A general rule of thumb in algebra is that you can do just about anything you want to one side of an equation, as long as you do the same thing to the other side (except divide or multiply by 0). Thus, **you can multiply or divide two complete equations together, because when you do so, you are doing the same thing to both sides of the equation**—by definition, both sides of an equation are equal.

What does it mean to multiply two equations together? It means that you multiply the left sides of the two equations together, and also multiply the right sides of the equations together. You then set those products equal to each other. To divide two equations, you take the same kinds of steps.

If $xy^2 = -96$ and $\dfrac{1}{xy} = \dfrac{1}{24}$, what is y?

While you could calculate the individual variables by solving for x or y first and substituting, if you simply multiply the equations together, you will quickly see that $y = -4$:

$$xy^2\left(\frac{1}{xy}\right) = -96\left(\frac{1}{24}\right) \qquad \frac{xy^2}{xy} = \frac{-96}{24} \qquad y = -4$$

If $\dfrac{a}{b} = 16$ and $\dfrac{a}{b^2} = 8$, what is ab?

Again, you could calculate the individual variables by solving for a first and substituting. But if you simply divide the first equation by the second, you will quickly see that $b = 2$:

$$\frac{\frac{a}{b}}{\frac{a}{b^2}} = \frac{16}{8} \qquad \frac{b^2 a}{ba} = 2 \qquad b = 2$$

You can then solve for a, and find that $ab = 64$:

$$\frac{a}{2} = 16 \qquad a = 16(2) = 32 \qquad ab = 32(2) = 64$$

Quadratic Formula

The vast majority of quadratic equations on the GMAT can be solved by the factoring or square-rooting techniques described in this chapter. However, very occasionally you might encounter a problem difficult to solve with these techniques. Such a problem requires an understanding of the quadratic formula, which can solve any quadratic equation but is cumbersome to use.

Quadratic Formula: **For any quadratic equation of the form $ax^2 + bx + c = 0$, where a, b, and c are constants, the solutions for x are given by:**

$$x = \frac{-b \pm \sqrt{b^2 - 4ac}}{2a}$$

Consider: If $x^2 + 8x + 13 = 0$, what is x?

This problem cannot be factored because there are no two integers for which the sum is 8 and the product is 13. However, you can find the solutions simply by plugging the coefficients from the equation into the quadratic formula:

$$x = \frac{-8 \pm \sqrt{8^2 - 4(1)(13)}}{2(1)} = \frac{-8 \pm \sqrt{64 - 52}}{2(1)} = -4 \pm \frac{\sqrt{12}}{2} = \{-4 + \sqrt{3}, -4 - \sqrt{3}\}$$

It is not imperative that you memorize the quadratic formula, but the expression underneath the radical in the formula ($\sqrt{b^2 - 4ac}$ called the **discriminant**) can convey important information: it can tell you how many solutions the equation has. If the discriminant is **greater than** zero, there will be two solutions. If the discriminant is **equal to** zero, there will be one solution. If the discriminant is **less than** zero, there will be **no** solutions, because you cannot take the square root of a negative number.

Which of the following equations has no solution for x?

(A) $x^2 - 8x - 11 = 0$
(B) $x^2 + 8x + 11 = 0$
(C) $x^2 + 7x + 11 = 0$
(D) $x^2 - 6x + 11 = 0$
(E) $x^2 - 6x - 11 = 0$

None of these equations can be solved by factoring. However, you can determine which of the equations has no solution by determining which equation has a negative discriminant (and note that you can stop at any point that you realize the answer will not be negative):

(A) $b^2 - 4ac = (-8)^2 - 4(1)(-11) = 64 + 44 = 108$ ⟵   For example, a positive plus a
(B) $b^2 - 4ac = (8)^2 - 4(1)(11) = 64 - 44 = 20$ positive will be positive, so you
(C) $b^2 - 4ac = (7)^2 - 4(1)(11) = 49 - 44 = 5$ could stop this calculation early.
(D) $b^2 - 4ac = (-6)^2 - 4(1)(11) = 36 - 44 = -8$
(E) $b^2 - 4ac = (-6)^2 - 4(1)(-11) = 36 + 44 = 80$

Therefore the equation in answer choice (D) has no solution. Again, **it is very rare for a GMAT problem to require familiarity with the quadratic formula.** The vast majority of quadratic equations can be factored through conventional methods.

Using Conjugates to Rationalize Denominators

Some GMAT problems involve fractions that contain square roots in the denominator. When the denominator is a square root alone, it is easy to simplify the fraction by simply multiplying the numerator and denominator by the square root:

Simplify $\dfrac{4}{\sqrt{2}}$.

By multiplying the numerator and denominator by the square root, you can remove the root from the denominator entirely:

$$\dfrac{4}{\sqrt{2}} \times \left(\dfrac{\sqrt{2}}{\sqrt{2}} \right) = \dfrac{4\sqrt{2}}{2} = 2\sqrt{2}$$

However, simplifying a denominator that contains the sum or difference of a square root *and* another term is more difficult:

Simplify $\dfrac{4}{3 - \sqrt{2}}$.

To simplify this type of problem, you need to use **the conjugate** of the denominator. The conjugate for any square root expression involving addition or subtraction is defined as follows:

For $a + \sqrt{b}$, the conjugate is given by $a - \sqrt{b}$.

For $a - \sqrt{b}$, the conjugate is given by $a + \sqrt{b}$.

In other words, simply change the sign of the square root term to find the conjugate. By multiplying the numerator and denominator by the conjugate, you eliminate the square root from the denominator:

$$\frac{4}{3-\sqrt{2}}\left(\frac{3+\sqrt{2}}{3+\sqrt{2}}\right) = \frac{4\left(3+\sqrt{2}\right)}{\left(3-\sqrt{2}\right)\left(3+\sqrt{2}\right)} = \frac{12+4\sqrt{2}}{9+3\sqrt{2}-3\sqrt{2}-2} = \frac{12+4\sqrt{2}}{7}$$

9

Problem Set

Solve each problem, applying the concepts and rules you learned in this section.

1. Given that $ab = 12$ and $\dfrac{c}{a} + 10 = 15$, what is bc?

2. If $|x + 1| = |3x - 2|$, what are the possible values for x?

    (A) 1/4 and 3/4
    (B) 1/4 and 3/2
    (C) 2/3 and 3/2
    (D) 2/3 and 4/3
    (E) 3/4 and 4/3

3. If $xy = 2$, $xz = 8$, and $yz = 5$, then the value of xyz is closest to:

    (A)   5
    (B)   9
    (C)   15
    (D)   25
    (E)   75

4. If $c + d = 11$ and c and d are positive integers, which of the following is a possible value for $5c + 8d$?

    (A)   55
    (B)   61
    (C)   69
    (D)   83
    (E)   88

5. If $mn = 3(m + 1) + n$ and m and n are integers, m could be any of the following values EXCEPT:

    (A)   2
    (B)   3
    (C)   4
    (D)   5
    (E)   7

6. Which of the following equations has no solution for a?

    (A) $a^2 - 6a + 7 = 0$
    (B) $a^2 + 6a - 7 = 0$
    (C) $a^2 + 4a + 3 = 0$
    (D) $a^2 - 4a + 3 = 0$
    (E) $a^2 - 4a + 5 = 0$

7. Which of the following is equal to $\dfrac{6 + \sqrt{5}}{2 - \sqrt{5}}$?

    (A) 17   (B) -17 (C) $17 + 8\sqrt{5}$ (D) $-17 - 8\sqrt{5}$ (E) $12 + 12\sqrt{5}$

P

Solutions

1. **60:**

$$\frac{c}{a} = 15 - 10 = 5$$

$$(ab)\left(\frac{c}{a}\right) = 12(5) \qquad bc = 12(5) = 60$$

You can first solve for $\frac{c}{a}$; then multiply the two equations together to quickly solve for bc.

2. **(B):** This is a complex absolute value problem, so you first must decide on an approach. The equation $|x + 1| = |3x - 2|$ has one variable (x) and several constants (1, 3, and −2). Thus, you should take an algebraic approach.

In theory, with two absolute value expressions you would set up four cases. However, those four cases collapse to just two cases: (1) the two expressions inside the absolute value symbols are given the same sign, and (2) the two expressions are given the opposite sign.

Case (1): Same Sign	Case (2): Opposite Sign
$x + 1 = 3x - 2$	$x + 1 = -(3x - 2) = -3x + 2$
$3 = 2x$	$4x = 1$
$x = \dfrac{3}{2}$	$x = \dfrac{1}{4}$

Testing each solution in the original equation, you verify that both solutions are valid:

$$\left|\frac{3}{2} + 1\right| = \left|3\left(\frac{3}{2}\right) - 2\right| \qquad \left|\frac{1}{4} + 1\right| = \left|3\left(\frac{1}{4}\right) - 2\right|$$

$$\left|\frac{5}{2}\right| = \left|\frac{9}{2} - 2\right| \qquad \left|\frac{5}{4}\right| = \left|\frac{3}{4} - 2\right| = \left|\frac{-5}{4}\right|$$

$$\frac{5}{2} = \frac{5}{2} \qquad \frac{5}{4} = \frac{5}{4}$$

3. **(B):** Multiplying together all three equations gives $x^2y^2z^2 = 80$. As a result, $xyz = \sqrt{80}$, which is very close to $xyz = 9$.

4. **(B):** Because c and d must be positive integers and $c + d = 11$, there are only ten possible values for $5c + 8d$ (starting with $c = 1$ and $d = 10$, then $c = 2$ and $d = 9$, and so on). In other words, if your starting point is $5c + 8d = 58$, where $c = 10$ and $d = 1$, if you reduce c by 1 and increase d by 1, the resulting sum will increase by 3; this pattern will continue to occur all the way to your largest possible value, 85. Starting with 58, then, keep adding 3 until you reach a number found in the answers. $58 + 3 = 61$, and 61 is one of the answer choices.

Alternatively, you can notice that consecutive values of $5c + 8d$ differ by 3. In other words, every possible value of $5c + 8d$ equals a multiple of 3 plus some constant. By inspection, you see that the values of $5c + 8d$ are all one more than a multiple of 3: for instance, the value $82 = 81 + 1$. The only answer choice that equals a multiple of 3 plus 1 is $61 = 60 + 1$.

5. **(D):** First, you need to solve for n. The reason you solve for n is that the answer choices list possible values for m, the other variable. If you solve for n, then you can plug the possible values for m into the formula and see when you get a non-integer for n, since n must be an integer:

$$mn = 3(m+1) + n$$
$$mn - n = 3(m+1)$$
$$n(m-1) = 3(m+1)$$
$$n = \frac{3(m+1)}{(m-1)} \longrightarrow$$

m	$n = \dfrac{3(m+1)}{(m-1)}$
2	$n = \dfrac{3(2+1)}{(2-1)} = 9$
3	$n = \dfrac{3(3+1)}{(3-1)} = 6$
4	$n = \dfrac{3(4+1)}{(4-1)} = 5$
5	$n = \dfrac{3(5+1)}{(5-1)} = \dfrac{18}{4} = \dfrac{9}{2}$
7	$n = \dfrac{3(7+1)}{(7-1)} = 4$

Only a value of 5 for m does not produce an integer for n.

6. **(E):** You can determine which of the equations has no solution by determining which equation has a negative discriminant:

(A) $b^2 - 4ac = (-6)^2 - 4(1)(7) = 36 - 28 = 8$
(B) $b^2 - 4ac = (6)^2 - 4(1)(-7) = 36 + 28 = 64$
(C) $b^2 - 4ac = (4)^2 - 4(1)(3) = 16 - 12 = 4$
(D) $b^2 - 4ac = (-4)^2 - 4(1)(3) = 16 - 12 = 4$
(E) $b^2 - 4ac = (-4)^2 - 4(1)(5) = 16 - 20 = -4$

7. **(D):** In order to simplify a fraction that has a difference involving a square root in the denominator, you need to multiply the numerator and denominator by the sum of the same terms (this is also known as the "conjugate"):

$$\frac{6+\sqrt{5}}{2-\sqrt{5}} = \frac{6+\sqrt{5}}{2-\sqrt{5}} \times \frac{2+\sqrt{5}}{2+\sqrt{5}} = \frac{\left(6+\sqrt{5}\right)\left(2+\sqrt{5}\right)}{2^2 - \left(\sqrt{5}\right)^2} = \frac{12 + 2\sqrt{5} + 6\sqrt{5} + 5}{4 - 5} = \frac{17 + 8\sqrt{5}}{-1} = -17 - 8\sqrt{5}$$

Chapter 10

Extra Functions Strategies

In This Chapter...

Chapter 10:

Extra Functions Strategies

Functions are very much like the "magic boxes" you may have learned about in elementary school.

> You put a 2 into the magic box, and a 7 comes out. You put a 3 into the magic box, and a 9 comes out. You put a 4 into the magic box, and an 11 comes out. What is the magic box doing to your number?

There are many possible ways to describe what the magic box is doing to your number. One possibility is as follows: The magic box is doubling your number and adding 3.

$$2(2) + 3 = 7 \qquad 2(3) + 3 = 9 \qquad 2(4) + 3 = 11$$

Assuming that this is the case (it is possible that the magic box is actually doing something different to your number), this description would yield the following "rule" for this magic box: $2x + 3$. This rule can be written in function form as:

$$f(x) = 2x + 3.$$

The function f represents the "rule" that the magic box is using to transform your number. Again, this rule may or may not be the "true" rule for the magic box. That is, if you put more numbers into the box and watch what numbers emerge, this rule may or may not hold. It is never possible to generalize a rule only by using specific cases.

Nevertheless, the magic box analogy is a helpful way to conceptualize a function as a *rule* built on an independent variable. The value of a function changes as the value of the independent variable changes. In other words, the value of a function is dependent on the value of the independent variable. Examples of functions include:

$f(x) = 4x^2 - 11$ The value of the function, f, is dependent on the independent variable, x.

$$g(t) = t^3 + \sqrt{t} - \frac{2t}{5}$$

The value of the function, g, is dependent on the independent variable, t.

You can think of functions as consisting of an "input" variable (the number you put into the magic box), and a corresponding "output" value (the number that comes out of the box). The function is simply the rule that turns the "input" variable into the "output" variable.

By the way, the expression $f(x)$ is pronounced "f of x", not "fx." It does *not* mean "f *times* x"! The letter f does *not* stand for a variable; rather, it stands for the rule that dictates how the input x changes into the output $f(x)$.

The "domain" of a function indicates the possible inputs. The "range" of a function indicates the possible outputs. For instance, the function $f(x) = x^2$ can take any input but never produces a negative number. So the domain is all numbers, but the range is $f(x) \geq 0$.

Numerical Substitution

This is the most basic type of function problem. Input the numerical value (say, 5) in place of the independent variable (x) to determine the value of the function.

If $f(x) = x^2 - 2$, what is the value of $f(5)$?

In this problem, you are given a rule for $f(x)$: square x and subtract 2. Then, you are asked to apply this rule to the number 5. Square 5 and subtract 2 from the result:

$$f(5) = (5)^2 - 2 = 25 - 2 = 23$$

Variable Substitution

This type of problem is slightly more complicated. Instead of finding the output value for a numerical input, you must find the output when the input is an algebraic expression.

If $f(z) = z^2 - \dfrac{z}{3}$, what is the value of $f(w + 6)$?

Input the variable expression ($w + 6$) in place of the independent variable (z) to determine the value of the function:

$$f(w + 6) = (w + 6)^2 - \frac{w + 6}{3}$$

MANHATTAN
GMAT

10

Compare this equation to the equation for $f(z)$. The expression $(w + 6)$ has taken the place of every z in the original equation. In a sense, you are treating the expression $(w + 6)$ as one thing, as if it were a single letter or variable.

The rest is algebraic simplification:

$$f(w+6) = (w+6)(w+6) - \left(\frac{w}{3} - \frac{6}{3}\right)$$
$$= w^2 + 12w + 36 - \frac{w}{3} - 2$$
$$= w^2 + 11\frac{2}{3}w + 34$$

Compound Functions

Imagine putting a number into one magic box, and then putting the output directly into another magic box. This is the situation you have with compound functions.

> If $f(x) = x^3 + \sqrt{x}$ and $g(x) = 4x - 3$, what is $f(g(3))$?

The expression $f(g(3))$, pronounced "f of g of 3", looks ugly, but the key to solving compound function problems is to work from the *inside out*. In this case, start with $g(3)$. Notice that we put the number into g, not into f, which may seem backward at first.

$$g(3) = 4(3) - 3 = 12 - 3 = 9$$

Use the result from the *inner* function g as the new input variable for the *outer* function f:

$$f(g(3)) = f(9) = (9)^3 + \sqrt{9} = 729 + 3 = 732 \qquad \text{The final result is 732.}$$

Note that changing the order of the compound functions changes the answer:

> If $f(x) = x^3 + \sqrt{x}$ and $g(x) = 4x - 3$, what is $g(f(3))$?

Again, work from the inside out. This time, start with $f(3)$ [which is now the inner function]:

$$f(3) = (3)^3 + \sqrt{3} = 27 + \sqrt{3}$$

Use the result from the *inner* function f as the new input variable for the *outer* function g:

$$g(f(3)) = g(27 + \sqrt{3}) = 4(27 + \sqrt{3}) - 3 = 108 + 4\sqrt{3} - 3 = 105 + 4\sqrt{3}$$

Thus, $g(f(3)) = 105 + 4\sqrt{3}$.

10

In general, $f(g(x))$ and $g(f(x))$ are **not the same rule overall** and will often lead to different outcomes. As an analogy, think of "putting on socks" and "putting on shoes" as two functions: the order in which you perform these steps obviously matters!

You may be asked to *find* a value of x for which $f(g(x)) = g(f(x))$. In that case, use *variable substitution*, working as always from the inside out:

If $f(x) = x^3 + 1$, and $g(x) = 2x$, for what value of x does $f(g(x)) = g(f(x))$?

Simply evaluate as we did in the problems above, using x instead of an input value:

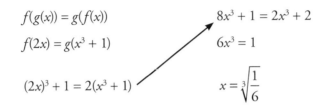

$$f(g(x)) = g(f(x)) \qquad\qquad 8x^3 + 1 = 2x^3 + 2$$
$$f(2x) = g(x^3 + 1) \qquad\qquad 6x^3 = 1$$
$$(2x)^3 + 1 = 2(x^3 + 1) \qquad\qquad x = \sqrt[3]{\frac{1}{6}}$$

Functions with Unknown Constants

On the GMAT, you may be given a function with an unknown constant. You will also be given the value of the function for a specific number. You can combine these pieces of information to find the complete function rule.

If $f(x) = ax^2 - x$, and $f(4) = 28$, what is $f(-2)$?

Solve these problems in three steps. *First*, use the value of the input variable and the corresponding output value of the function to solve for the unknown constant:

$$f(4) = a(4)^2 - 4 = 28$$
$$16a - 4 = 28$$
$$16a = 32$$
$$a = 2$$

Then, rewrite the function, replacing the constant with its numerical value:

$$f(x) = ax^2 - x = 2x^2 - x$$

Finally, solve the function for the new input variable:

$$f(-2) = 2(-2)^2 - (-2) = 8 + 2 = 10$$

Function Graphs

A function can be visualized by graphing it in the coordinate plane. The input variable is considered the domain of the function, or the x-coordinate. The corresponding output is considered the range of the function, or the y-coordinate.

What is the graph of the function $f(x) = -2x^2 + 1$?

Create an INPUT–OUTPUT table by evaluating the function for several input values:

INPUT	OUTPUT	(x, y)
–2	$-2(-2)^2 + 1 = -7$	$(-2, -7)$
–1	$-2(-1)^2 + 1 = -1$	$(-1, -1)$
0	$-2(0)^2 + 1 = 1$	$(0, 1)$
1	$-2(1)^2 + 1 = -1$	$(1, -1)$
2	$-2(2)^2 + 1 = -7$	$(2, -7)$

Then, plot points to see the shape of the graph:

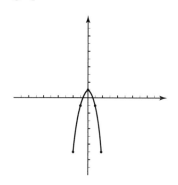

It may be sufficient to calculate only 3 or 4 values as long as you have found the pattern and can accurately represent the graph. For more on graphing functions, see the "Coordinate Plane" chapter of the Manhattan GMAT *Geometry* Strategy Guide.

Common Function Types

Though the GMAT could pose function questions in many different forms, several different themes occur through many of them. This section explores some of these common types of functions.

Proportionality

Many GMAT problems, especially those concerned with real-life situations, will use direct or inverse proportionality between the input and the output values. These special functions are defined as follows.

Direct proportionality means that the two quantities always change by the same factor and in the same direction. For instance, tripling the input will cause the output to triple as well. Cutting the input in half will also cut the output in half. Direct proportionality relationships are of the form $y = kx$, where x is the input value and y is the output value. k is called the **proportionality constant**. This equation can also be written as $\frac{y}{x} = k$, which means that the ratio of the output and input values is always constant.

> The maximum height reached by an object thrown directly upward is directly proportional to the square of the velocity with which the object is thrown. If an object thrown upward at 16 feet per second reaches a maximum height of 4 feet, with what speed must the object be thrown upward to reach a maximum height of 9 feet?

Typically with direct proportion problems, you will be given "before" and "after" values. Simply set up ratios to solve the problem. For example, $\dfrac{y_1}{x_1}$ can be used for the "before" values and $\dfrac{y_2}{x_2}$ can be used for the "after" values. You then write $\dfrac{y_1}{x_1} = \dfrac{y_2}{x_2}$, since both ratios are equal to the same constant k. Finally, you solve for the unknowns.

In the problem given above, be sure to note that the direct proportion is between the height and the square of the velocity, not the velocity itself. Therefore, write the proportion as $\dfrac{h_1}{v_1^{\,2}} = \dfrac{h_2}{v_2^{\,2}}$. Substitute the known values $h_1 = 4$, $v_1 = 16$, and $h_2 = 9$:

$$\frac{4}{16^2} = \frac{9}{v_2^{\,2}} \qquad v_2^{\,2} = 9\left(\frac{16^2}{4}\right) \qquad v_2^{\,2} = 9(64) = 576 \qquad v_2 = 24$$

The object must be thrown upward at 24 feet per second.

Inverse proportionality means that the two quantities change by *reciprocal* factors. Cutting the input in half will actually double the output. Tripling the input will cut the output to one-third of its original value.

Inverse proportionality relationships are of the form $y = \dfrac{k}{x}$, where x is the input value and y is the output value. k is called the **proportionality constant**. This equation can also be written as $xy = k$, which means that the product of the output and input values is always constant.

As with other proportion problems, you will typically be given "before" and "after" values. However, this time you set up **products**, not ratios, to solve the problem—for example, $y_1 x_1$ can be used for the "before" values and $y_2 x_2$ can be used for the "after" values. Next, write $y_1 x_1 = y_2 x_2$, since each product equals the same constant k. Finally, use algebra to solve for the unknowns in the problem.

> The amount of electrical current that flows through a wire is inversely proportional to the resistance in that wire. If a wire currently carries 4 amperes of electrical current, but the resistance is then cut to one-third of its original value, how many amperes of electrical current will flow through the wire?

While you are not given precise amounts for the "before" or "after" resistance in the wire, you can pick numbers. Using 3 as the original resistance and 1 as the new resistance, you can see that the new electrical current will be 12 amperes:

$$C_1R_1 = C_2R_2 \qquad 4(3) = C_2(1) \qquad 12 = C_2$$

Linear Growth

Many GMAT problems, especially word problems, feature quantities with **linear growth** (or decay) that is, they grow at a constant rate. Such quantities are determined by the linear function: $y = mx + b$. In this equation, the slope m is the constant rate at which the quantity grows. The y-intercept b is the value of the quantity at time zero, and the variable (in this case, x) stands for time. You can also use t to represent time.

For instance, if a baby weighs 9 pounds at birth and gains 1.2 pounds per month, then the baby's weight can be written as $W = 9 + 1.2t$, where t is the baby's age in months. Note that $t = 0$ represents the birth of the baby.

> Jake was 4½ feet tall on his 12th birthday, when he began to have a growth spurt. Between his 12th and 15th birthdays, he grew at a constant rate. If Jake was 20% taller on his 15th birthday than on his 13th birthday, how many inches per year did Jake grow during his growth spurt? (12 inches = 1 foot)

In this problem, the constant growth does not begin until Jake has reached his twelfth birthday, so in order to use the constant growth function $y = mx + b$, let time $x = 0$ (the initial state) stand for Jake's twelfth birthday. Therefore, $x = 1$ stands for his 13th birthday, $x = 2$ stands for his 14th birthday, and $x = 3$ stands for his 15th birthday.

The problem asks for an answer in inches but gives you information in feet. Therefore, it is convenient to convert to inches at the beginning of the problem: 4½ feet = 54 inches = b. Since the growth rate m is unknown, the growth function can be written as $y = mx + 54$. Jake's height on his 13th birthday, when $x = 1$, was $54 + m$, and his height on his 15th birthday, when $x = 3$, was $54 + 3m$, which is 20% more than $54 + m$. Thus, you have:

$$54 + 3m = (54 + m) + 0.20(54 + m) \qquad 1.8m = 10.8$$
$$54 + 3m = 1.2(54 + m) \qquad\qquad m = 6$$
$$54 + 3m = 64.8 + 1.2m$$

Therefore, Jake grew at a rate of 6 inches each year.

10

Uncommon Function Types

Exponential Growth

Although not as common as linear growth, **exponential growth** also appears occasionally on GMAT problems. In exponential growth, a quantity is multiplied by the same constant each period of time (rather than adding the same constant, as in linear growth). Any exponential growth can be written as $y(t) = y_0 \cdot k^t$, in which y represents the quantity as a function of time t, y_0 is the value of the quantity at time $t = 0$, and k represents the constant multiplier for one period. Commonly, exponential growth multipliers take the form of percentage multipliers. For instance, for a quantity that increases by 7% each period, $k = 1.07$.

Notice the similarity between this formula for exponential growth and the formula for an exponential sequence ($S_n = xk^n$), where x and k are constants. The difference is that with $y(t) = y_0 \cdot k^t$, the variable t can take on non-integer values. In a sequence, n must be an integer, typically 1 or greater.

> A quantity increases in a manner such that the ratio of its values in any two consecutive years is constant. If the quantity doubles every 6 years, by what factor does it increase in two years?

There are a couple of phrases to notice in this problem. First, "...such that the ratio of its values in any two consecutive years is constant" implies exponential growth, so the quantity can be represented by the function $y(t) = y_0 \cdot k^t$. Second, "by what factor" refers to a multiplier of the original quantity.

The value of the quantity at time zero ($t = 0$) is y_0. Because the quantity doubles every 6 years, its value at time $t = 6$ years must be $2y_0$. Therefore:

$$2y_0 = y_0(k^6) \qquad\qquad 2 = k^6 \quad \text{(notice that } y_0 \text{ cancels out)} \qquad\qquad \sqrt[6]{2} = k$$

The factor by which the quantity increases in two years ($t = 2$) is $k^2 = \sqrt[6]{2^2} = \sqrt[3]{2}$.

For more on Exponential Growth, see the "Rates & Work" chapter of the Manhattan GMAT *Word Problems* Strategy Guide.

Symmetry

Some difficult GMAT function questions revolve around "symmetry," or the property that two seemingly different inputs to the function always yield the same output.

For which of the following functions does $f(x) = f\left(\dfrac{1}{x}\right)$, given that $x \neq -2, -1, 0,$ or 1?

(A) $f(x) = \left|\dfrac{x+1}{x}\right|$ (B) $f(x) = \left|\dfrac{x+1}{x-1}\right|$ (C) $f(x) = \left|\dfrac{x-1}{x}\right|$

(D) $f(x) = \left|\dfrac{x}{x+1}\right|$ (E) $f(x) = \left|\dfrac{x+1}{x+2}\right|$

There are two primary ways that you can set about solving this problem. First, you could substitute $\dfrac{1}{x}$ in for x in each of the functions and simplify, to see which of the functions yields the same result. Alternatively, you could pick a number for x and see which of the functions produces an equal output for both x and $\dfrac{1}{x}$. In most cases, the latter strategy will probably be easier. For example, you could choose $x = 3$:

		$f(3)$	$f\left(\dfrac{1}{3}\right)$
(A)	$f(x) = \left\|\dfrac{x+1}{x}\right\|$	$\left\|\dfrac{3+1}{3}\right\| = \dfrac{4}{3}$	$\left\|\dfrac{\frac{1}{3}+1}{\frac{1}{3}}\right\| = \dfrac{\frac{4}{3}}{\frac{1}{3}} = 4$
(B)	$f(x) = \left\|\dfrac{x+1}{x-1}\right\|$	$\left\|\dfrac{3+1}{3-1}\right\| = \dfrac{4}{2} = 2$	$\left\|\dfrac{\frac{1}{3}+1}{\frac{1}{3}-1}\right\| = \dfrac{\frac{4}{3}}{-\frac{2}{3}} = 2$
(C)	$f(x) = \left\|\dfrac{x-1}{x}\right\|$	$\left\|\dfrac{3-1}{3}\right\| = \dfrac{2}{3}$	$\left\|\dfrac{\frac{1}{3}-1}{\frac{1}{3}}\right\| = \dfrac{-\frac{2}{3}}{\frac{1}{3}} = 2$
(D)	$f(x) = \left\|\dfrac{x}{x+1}\right\|$	$\left\|\dfrac{3}{3+1}\right\| = \dfrac{3}{4}$	$\left\|\dfrac{\frac{1}{3}}{\frac{1}{3}+1}\right\| = \dfrac{\frac{1}{3}}{\frac{4}{3}} = \dfrac{1}{4}$
(E)	$f(x) = \left\|\dfrac{x+1}{x+2}\right\|$	$\left\|\dfrac{3+1}{3+2}\right\| = \dfrac{4}{5}$	$\left\|\dfrac{\frac{1}{3}+1}{\frac{1}{3}+2}\right\| = \dfrac{\frac{4}{3}}{\frac{7}{3}} = \dfrac{4}{7}$

10

Only (B) returns the same result for 3 and $\dfrac{1}{3}$, so it is the correct answer. Note that, if you are confident with your math, you can stop after testing (B) and realizing that it does work. You can also prove that (B) is the correct answer algebraically:

$$f(x) = \left|\frac{x+1}{x-1}\right|$$

$$f\left(\frac{1}{x}\right) = \left|\frac{\frac{1}{x}+1}{\frac{1}{x}-1}\right| = \left|\frac{\frac{x+1}{x}}{\frac{1-x}{x}}\right| = \left|\frac{x+1}{1-x}\right| = \left|\frac{x+1}{-(1-x)}\right| = \left|\frac{x+1}{x-1}\right|$$

Properties

Other advanced function problems on the GMAT test whether certain functions follow certain properties of mathematics. For example:

For which of the following functions does $f(x-y)$ NOT EQUAL $f(x) - f(y)$?

For which of the following functions does $f(a(b+c)) = f(ab) + f(ac)$?

For all of these questions a quick, effective approach is simply to pick numbers and see which function gives the desired result.

10

Problem Set

1.   If $f(x) = 2x^4 - x^2$, what is the value of $f(2\sqrt{3})$?

2.   If $g(x) = 3x + \sqrt{x}$, what is the value of $g(d^2 + 6d + 9)$?

3.   If $k(x) = 4x^3a$, and $k(3) = 27$, what is $k(2)$?

4.   If $f(x) = 2x^2 - 4$ and $g(x) = 2x$, for what values of x will $f(x) = g(x)$?

5.   If $f(x) = (x + \sqrt{3})^4$, what is the range of the function $f(x)$?

     (A) $\sqrt{3} < f(x) < 4$ (B) $f(x) \geq 0$ (C) $f(x) < 0$ (D) $f(x) \neq 0$

6.   If $g(x) = \dfrac{x^3 - ax}{4}$, and $g(2) = \dfrac{1}{2}$, what is the value of $g(4)$?

7.   The velocity of a falling object in a vacuum is directly proportional to the amount of time the object has been falling. If after 5 seconds an object is falling at a speed of 90 miles per hour, how fast will it be falling after 12 seconds?

8.   The "luminous flux," or perceived brightness, of a light source is measured in lumens and is inversely proportional to the square of the distance from the light. If a light source produces 200 lumens at a distance of 3 meters, at what distance will the light source produce a luminous flux of 25 lumens?

9.   A strain of bacteria multiplies such that the ratio of its population in any two consecutive minutes is constant. If the bacteria grows from a population of 5 million to a population of 40 million in one hour, by what factor does the population increase every 10 minutes?

10. For which of the following functions does $f(x) = f(2 - x)$?

     (A) $f(x) = x + 2$
     (B) $f(x) = 2x - x^2$
     (C) $f(x) = 2 - x$
     (D) $f(x) = (2 - x)^2$
     (E) $f(x) = x^2$

Solutions

1. **276:**

$$f(x) = 2\left(2\sqrt{3}\right)^4 - \left(2\sqrt{3}\right)^2$$
$$= 2(2)^4\left(\sqrt{3}\right)^4 - (2)^2\left(\sqrt{3}\right)^2$$
$$= (2 \times 16 \times 9) - (4 \times 3)$$
$$= 288 - 12 = 276$$

2. **$3d^2 + 19d + 30$ OR $3d^2 + 17d + 24$:**

$$g(d^2 + 6d + 9) = 3(d^2 + 6d + 9) + \sqrt{d^2 + 6d + 9}$$
$$= 3d^2 + 18d + 27 + \sqrt{(d+3)^2}$$
$$= 3d^2 + 18d + 27 + d + 3 \qquad \text{OR} \qquad 3d^2 + 18d + 27 - (d + 3)$$
$$= 3d^2 + 19d + 30 \qquad\qquad \text{OR} \qquad 3d^2 + 17d + 24$$
$$\text{(if } d + 3 > 0) \qquad\qquad\qquad \text{(if } d + 3 < 0)$$

3. **8:** $k(3) = 27$ Therefore,

$$4(3)^3 a = 27 \qquad k(x) = 4x^3\left(\frac{1}{4}\right) = x^3 \quad \longrightarrow \quad k(2) = (2)^3 = 8$$
$$4(27)a = 27$$
$$4a = 1$$
$$a = \frac{1}{4}$$

4. **{–1, 2}:** To find the values for which $f(x) = g(x)$, set the functions equal to each other.

$$2x^2 - 4 = 2x$$
$$2x^2 - 2x - 4 = 0$$
$$2(x^2 - x - 2) = 0$$
$$2(x - 2)(x + 1) = 0$$

$$x - 2 = 0 \qquad \text{OR} \qquad x + 1 = 0$$
$$x = 2 \qquad\qquad\qquad x = -1$$

5. **(B):** If $f(x) = (x + \sqrt{3})^4$, the range of outputs, or y-values, can never be negative. Regardless of the value of x, raising $x + \sqrt{3}$ to an even power will result in a non-negative y-value. Therefore, the range of the function is all non-negative numbers, or $f(x) \geq 0$.

6. **13:** $g(2) = \dfrac{(2)^3 - a(2)}{4} = \dfrac{1}{2}$

$$8 - 2a = 2$$

P

$$2a = 6 \quad \rightarrow \quad g(x) = \frac{x^3 - 3x}{4} \quad \rightarrow \quad g(4) = \frac{(4)^3 - 3(4)}{4} = \frac{\cancel{4}(4^2 - 3(1))}{\cancel{4}} = \frac{16 - 3}{1} = 13$$

$$a = 3$$

7. **216 miles per hour:** Because the velocity and the time spent falling are directly proportional, you can simply set the ratio of the "before" velocity and time to the "after" velocity and time:

$$\frac{v_1}{w_1} = \frac{v_2}{w_2}$$

$$\frac{90 \text{ mph}}{5 \text{ sec}} = \frac{v_2}{12 \text{ sec}}$$

$$v_2 = \frac{90(12)}{5} = 216 \text{ mph}$$

8. **$6\sqrt{2}$ meters or $\sqrt{72}$ meters:** Because the intensity of the light source and the *square* of the distance are inversely proportional, you can write the product of the "before" intensity and distance squared and the product of the "after" intensity and distance squared. Then set these two products equal to each other:

$$I_1 \times d_1^2 = I_2 \times d_2^2$$

$$(200 \text{ lumens})(3 \text{ meters})^2 = (25 \text{ lumens}) \times d_2^2$$

$$d_2^2 = \frac{(200 \text{ lumens})(3 \text{ meters})^2}{(25 \text{ lumens})}$$

$$d_2 = 6\sqrt{2} \text{ meters}$$

9. **$\sqrt{2}$:** This is an exponential growth problem, so you should use the equation $y(t) = y_0 \cdot k^t$. In one hour (60 minutes), the population grows by a factor of $\frac{40,000,000}{5,000,000} = 8$, which also equals k^{60}. Thus, in one minute, the population grows by a factor of $k = \sqrt[60]{8} = \sqrt[60]{2^3} = \sqrt[20]{2}$. The question asks what factor the population will grow by in 10 minutes, so simply take this factor to the tenth power: $k^{10} = \left(\sqrt[20]{2}\right)^{10} = \sqrt{2}$.

Alternatively, you could notice that $8 = 2^3$, so an hour equals 3 periods of doubling. In other words, the population doubles every 20 minutes. In 10 minutes, therefore, the population increases by a factor of $\sqrt{2}$. (In this way, two periods of 10 minutes lead to an increase by a factor of $\sqrt{2} \times \sqrt{2} = 2$.)

10. **(B):** This is a "symmetry function" type of problem. Generally the easiest way to solve these kinds of problems is to pick numbers and plug them into each function to determine which answer gives the desired result. For example, you could pick $x = 4$:

		$f(4)$	$f(2 - 4)$
(A)	$f(x) = x + 2$	$4 + 2 = 6$	$(2 - 4) + 2 = 0$
(B)	$f(x) = 2x - x^2$	$2(4) - 4^2 = -8$	$2(2 - 4) - (2 - 4)^2 =$ $-4 - 4 = -8$
(C)	$f(x) = 2 - x$	$2 - 4 = -2$	$2 - (2 - 4) = 4$
(D)	$f(x) = (2 - x)^2$	$(2 - 4)^2 = 4$	$[2 - (2 - 4)]^2 = 4^2 = 16$
(E)	$f(x) = x^2$	$4^2 = 16$	$(2 - 4)^2 = 4$

P

Chapter 11

of Algebra

Extra Inequalities Strategies

In This Chapter...

Chapter 11:
Extra Inequalities Strategies

Optimization Problems

Related to extreme values are problems involving optimization: specifically, minimization or maximization problems. In these problems, you need to **focus on the largest and smallest possible values for each of the variables**, as some combination of them will usually lead to the largest or smallest possible result.

> If $2y + 3 \leq 11$ and $1 \leq x \leq 5$, what is the maximum possible value for xy?

You need to test the extreme values for x and for y to determine which combinations of extreme values will maximize xy:

$$2y + 3 \leq 11 \qquad 2y \leq 8 \qquad y \leq 4$$

Extreme Values for x	**Extreme Values for y**
The lowest value for x is 1.	There is no lower limit to y.
The highest value for x is 5.	The highest value for y is 4.

Now consider the different extreme value scenarios for x, y, and xy:

Since y has no lower limit and x is positive, the product xy has no lower limit.

Using y's highest value (4), test the extreme values of x (1 and 5). The first extreme value generates a product $xy = (1)(4) = 4$. The second extreme value generates $xy = (5)(4) = 20$.

Clearly, xy is maximized when $x = 5$ and $y = 4$, with a result that $xy = 20$.

> If $-7 \leq a \leq 6$ and $-7 \leq b \leq 8$, what is the maximum possible value for ab?

Once again, you are looking for a maximum possible value, this time for *ab*. You need to test the extreme values for *a* and for *b* to determine which combinations of extreme values will maximize *ab*:

Extreme Values for *a*	**Extreme Values for *b***
The lowest value for *a* is –7.	The lowest value for *b* is –7.
The highest value for *a* is 6.	The highest value for *b* is 8.

Now consider the different extreme value scenarios for *a*, *b*, and *ab*:

a		*b*		*ab*
Min	–7	Min	–7	$(-7) \times (-7) = \mathbf{49}$
Min	–7	Max	8	$(-7) \times 8 = -56$
Max	6	Min	–7	$6 \times (-7)$
Max	6	Max	8	$6 \times 8 = 48$

This time, *ab* is maximized when you take the *negative* extreme values for both *a* and *b*, resulting in *ab* = 49. Notice that you could have focused right away on the first and fourth scenarios, because they are the only scenarios which produce positive products.

Reciprocals of Inequalities

Taking reciprocals of inequalities is similar to multiplying/dividing by negative numbers. You need to consider the positive/negative cases of the variables involved. The general rule is that **if *x* < *y*, then:**

- $\dfrac{1}{x} > \dfrac{1}{y}$ **when *x* and *y* are positive.** Flip the inequality. If $3 < 5$, then $\dfrac{1}{3} > \dfrac{1}{5}$.

- $\dfrac{1}{x} > \dfrac{1}{y}$ **when *x* and *y* are negative.** Flip the inequality. If $-4 < -2$, then $\dfrac{1}{-4} > \dfrac{1}{-2}$.

- $\dfrac{1}{x} < \dfrac{1}{y}$ **when *x* is negative and *y* is positive.** Do *not* flip the inequality.

  If $-6 < 7$, then $\dfrac{1}{-6} < \dfrac{1}{7}$. The left side is negative, while the right side is positive.

- **If you do not know the sign of *x* or *y*, you cannot take reciprocals.**

In summary, if you know the signs of the variables, you should flip the inequality *unless* *x* and *y* have different signs.

Given that $ab < 0$ and $a > b$, which of the following must be true?

    I. $a > 0$
    II. $b > 0$
    III. $\dfrac{1}{a} > \dfrac{1}{b}$

(A) I only
(B) II only
(C) I and III only
(D) II and III only
(E) I, II and III

You know from the problem stem that $ab < 0$ and $a > b$. This tells you that a and b have different signs, so a must be positive and b must be negative. Therefore I is true, while II is not true.

You also know from the discussion on reciprocals that if $a > b$, then $\dfrac{1}{a} < \dfrac{1}{b}$ (the inequality is flipped)

Unless a and b have different signs, in which case $\dfrac{1}{a} > \dfrac{1}{b}$. Since a and b have different signs here, $\dfrac{1}{a} > \dfrac{1}{b}$.

Therefore the correct answer is (C).

Squaring Inequalities

As with reciprocals, you cannot square both sides of an inequality unless you know the signs of both sides of the inequality. However, the rules for squaring inequalities are somewhat different from those for reciprocating inequalities.

- **If both sides are known to be negative, then flip the inequality sign when you square.** For instance, if $x < -3$, then the left side must be negative. Since both sides are negative, you can square both sides and reverse the inequality sign: $x^2 > 9$. However, if you are given an inequality such as $x > -3$, then you cannot square both sides, because it is unclear whether the left side is positive or negative. If x is negative, then $x^2 < 9$, but if x is positive, then x^2 could be either greater than 9 or less than 9.

- **If both sides are known to be positive, then do not flip the inequality sign when you square.** For instance, if $x > 3$, then the left side must be positive; since both sides are positive, you can square both sides to yield $x^2 > 9$. If you are given an inequality such as $x < 3$, however, then you cannot square both sides, because it is unclear whether the left side is positive or negative. If x is positive, then $x^2 < 9$, but if x is negative, then x^2 could be either greater than 9 or less than 9.

11

- **If one side is positive and one side is negative, then you cannot square.** For example, if you know that $x < y$, x is negative, and y is positive, you cannot make any determination about x^2 vs. y^2. If, for example, $x = -2$ and $y = 2$, then $x^2 = y^2$. If $x = -2$ and $y = 3$, then $x^2 < y^2$. If $x = -2$ and $y = 1$, then $x^2 > y^2$. It should be noted that if one side of the inequality is negative and the other side is positive, then squaring is probably not warranted—some other technique is likely needed to solve the problem.

- **If the signs are unclear, then you cannot square.** Put simply, you would not know whether to flip the sign of the inequality once you have squared it.

    Is $x^2 > y^2$?

    (1) $x > y$
    (2) $x > 0$

In this problem, you need to know whether $x^2 > y^2$. Statement 1 is insufficient, because you do not know whether x and y are positive or negative numbers. For example, if $x = 5$ and $y = 4$, then $x^2 > y^2$. However, if $x = -4$ and $y = -5$, then $x > y$ but $x^2 < y^2$.

Statement 2 does not tell you anything about y, so it too is insufficient.

Combined, you know that x is positive and larger than y. This is still insufficient, because y could be a negative number of larger magnitude than x. For example, if $x = 3$ and $y = 2$, then $x^2 > y^2$, but if $x = 3$ and $y = -4$, then $x^2 < y^2$. Therefore, the correct answer is (E).

11

Problem Set

1.   If *a* and *b* are integers and $-4 \leq a \leq 3$ and $-4 \leq b \leq 5$, what is the maximum possible value for *ab*?

2.   Is $mn > -12$?

     (1) $m > -3$
     (2) $n > -4$

3.   If $\dfrac{4}{x} < \dfrac{1}{3}$, what is the possible range of values for *x*?

4.   If $\dfrac{4}{x} < -\dfrac{1}{3}$, what is the possible range of values for *x*?

5.   Is $x < y$?

     (1) $\dfrac{1}{x} < \dfrac{1}{y}$

     (2) $\dfrac{x}{y} < 0$

P

Solutions

1. **16:** In order to maximize ab, you need to test the endpoints of the ranges for a and b:

> If $a = -4$ and $b = -4$, $ab = 16$.
> If $a = -4$ and $b = 5$, the product is negative (smaller than 16).
> If $a = 3$ and $b = -4$, the product is negative (smaller than 16).
> If $a = 3$ and $b = 5$, $ab = 15$.

Thus the maximum value for ab is 16. Notice that this maximum occurs when a and b are both negative in this case.

2. **(E):** Combining the two statements, it is tempting to conclude that mn must either be positive or a negative number larger than -12. However, because either variable could be positive or negative, it is possible to end up with a negative number less than -12. For example, m could equal -1 and n could equal 50. In that case, $mn = -50$, which is less than -12. Therefore, the two statements combined are INSUFFICIENT. The correct answer is (E).

3. **$x < 0$ OR $x > 12$:** For this type of problem, you have to consider two possibilities: x could be positive or negative. When you multiply the inequality by x, you will need to flip the sign when x is negative, but not flip the sign when x is positive:

Case 1: $x > 0$	**Case 2: $x < 0$**
$\dfrac{4}{x} < \dfrac{1}{3}$	$\dfrac{4}{x} > \dfrac{1}{3}$
$12 < x$	$12 > x$

For Case 1, x must be positive AND greater than 12. Thus, $x > 12$.

For Case 2, x must be negative AND less than 12. Thus, $x < 0$.

Combined, $x < 0$ OR $x > 12$.

4. **$-12 < x < 0$:** For this type of problem, you have to consider two possibilities: x could be positive or negative. When you multiply the inequality by x, you will need to flip the sign when x is negative, but not flip the sign when x is positive. However, notice that x *cannot* be positive: the left-hand side of the inequality is less than $-\dfrac{1}{3}$, which means $\dfrac{4}{x}$ must be negative. Therefore x must be negative:

Case 1: $x > 0$	**Case 2: $x < 0$**
Not Possible	$\dfrac{4}{x} < -\dfrac{1}{3}$
	$12 > -x$
	$-12 < x$

P

Case 1 is not possible.

For Case 2, x must be negative AND greater than -12. Thus, $-12 < x < 0$.

5. **(C):** The meaning of Statement (1) depends on the signs of x and y. If x and y are either both positive or both negative, then you can take reciprocals of both sides, yielding $x > y$. However, this statement could also be true if x is negative and y is positive; in that case, $x < y$. INSUFFICIENT.

Statement (2) tells you that the quotient of x and y is negative. In that case, x and y have different signs: one is positive and the other is negative. However, this does not tell you which one is positive and which one is negative. INSUFFICIENT.

Combining the two statements, if you know that the reciprocal of x is less than that of y, and that x and y have opposite signs, then x must be negative and y must be positive, so $x < y$. SUFFICIENT. The correct answer is (C).

P

Appendix A
of
Algebra

Official Guide Problem Sets

In This Chapter...

Official Guide Problem Sets

Problem Solving Set

Data Sufficiency Set

Official Guide Problem Sets

Now that you have completed *Algebra*, it is time to test your skills on problems that have actually appeared on real GMAT exams over the past several years.

The problem sets that follow are composed of questions from two books published by the Graduate Management Admission Council® (the organization that develops the official GMAT exam):

> *The Official Guide for GMAT Review, 13th Edition*
> *The Official Guide for GMAT Quantitative Review, 2nd Edition*

These books contain quantitative questions that have appeared on past official GMAT exams. (The questions contained therein are the property of The Graduate Management Admission Council, which is not affiliated in any way with Manhattan GMAT.)

Although the questions in *The Official Guides* have been "retired" (they will not appear on future official GMAT exams), they are great practice questions.

In order to help you practice effectively, we have categorized every problem in *The Official Guides* by topic and subtopic. On the following pages, you will find two categorized lists:

> 1. **Problem Solving:**   Lists Problem Solving Algebra questions contained in
>   *The Official Guides* and categorizes them by subtopic.
>
> 2. **Data Sufficiency:**   Lists Data Sufficiency Algebra questions contained in
>   *The Official Guides* and categorizes them by subtopic.

Books 1 through 8 of Manhattan GMAT's Strategy Guide series each contain a unique *Official Guide* list that pertains to the specific topic of that particular book. If you complete all the practice problems contained on the *Official Guide* lists in each of these 8 Manhattan GMAT Strategy Guide books, you will have completed every single question published in *The Official Guides*.

Problem Solving Set

This set is from *The Official Guide for GMAT Review, 13th Edition* (pages 20–23 & 152–185), and *The Official Guide for GMAT Quantitative Review, 2nd Edition* (pages 62–86).

Solve each of the following problems in a notebook, making sure to demonstrate how you arrived at each answer by showing all of your work and computations. If you get stuck on a problem, look back at the Algebra strategies and content contained in this guide to assist you.

Note: Problem numbers preceded by "D" refer to questions in the Diagnostic Test chapter of *The Official Guide for GMAT Review, 13th Edition* (pages 20–23).

Linear Equations:

> *13th Edition:* 14, 42, 47, 54, 55, 72, 102, 187, 220
> *Quantitative Review:* 2, 40, 41, 99, 107, 111

Exponents & Roots:

> *13th Edition:* 9, 35, 52, 106, 120, 150, 164, 180, 196, 217, 230, D17
> *Quantitative Review:* 36, 47, 74, 86, 96, 97, 106, 108, 147, 163, 166, 170

Quadratic Equations:

> *13th Edition:* 37, 45, 99, 117, 157, 169, 191, 199, 216, 223, D16
> *Quantitative Review:* 20, 57, 72, 103, 121, 133

Formulas:

> *13th Edition:* 70, 100, 126, 129, 134, 149, 160, 190, D3
> *Quantitative Review:* 1, 28, 67, 77, 91, 113, 131, 144, 158

Inequalities:

> *13th Edition:* 50, 73, 130, 138, 143, 176, 192
> *Quantitative Review:* 5, 92, 105, 156

Data Sufficiency Set

This set is from *The Official Guide for GMAT Review, 13th Edition* (pages 24–26 & 274–291), and *The Official Guide for GMAT Quantitative Review, 2nd Edition* (pages 152–163).

Solve each of the following problems in a notebook, making sure to demonstrate how you arrived at each answer by showing all of your work and computations. If you get stuck on a problem, look back at the Algebra strategies and content contained in this guide to assist you.

Practice **rephrasing** both the questions and the statements. The majority of data sufficiency problems can be rephrased; however, if you have difficulty rephrasing a problem, try testing numbers to solve it. It is especially important that you familiarize yourself with the directions for data sufficiency problems, and that you memorize the 5 fixed answer choices that accompany all data sufficiency problems.

Note: Problem numbers preceded by "D" refer to questions in the Diagnostic Test chapter of *The Official Guide for GMAT Review, 13th Edition* (pages 24–26).

Linear Equations:

> *13th Edition:* 1, 17, 36, 60, 86, 98, 136, 156, 171, D35, D37
> *Quantitative Review:* 15, 23, 35, 57, 61, 80, 94, 106, 124

Exponents & Roots:

> *13th Edition:* 15, 41, 53, 160, 162, 169, 172, D44
> *Quantitative Review:* 18, 25, 28, 31, 54, 76, 79, 81, 100, 109, 110, 113, 121

Quadratic Equations:

> *13th Edition:* 67, 99, 163
> *Quantitative Review:* 37, 46, 62, 73, 83

Formulas:

> *13th Edition:* 24, 96, 118
> *Quantitative Review:* 107, 111

Inequalities:

> *13th Edition:* 13, 33, 43, 48, 50, 52, 82, 85, 100, 159, 167, D30, D33, D38
> *Quantitative Review:* 32, 40, 42, 51, 52, 56, 68, 69, 89, 120